THE
LITTLE
BOOK
OF
ENGLAND

STUART LAYCOCK
AND PHILIP LAYCOCK

First published 2023

The History Press
97 St George's Place, Cheltenham,
Gloucestershire, GL50 3QB
www.thehistorypress.co.uk

British Library Cataloguing in Publication Data.
A catalogue record for this book is available from the British Library.

ISBN 978 1 80399 197 9

Typesetting and origination by The History Press
Printed and bound in Great Britain by TJ Books Limited, Padstow, Cornwall.

Trees for LYfe

CONTENTS

A LITTLE (VERY LITTLE) INTRODUCTION

England is, of course, a huge subject. OK, it's not huge in the sense of a huge landmass or a huge (by world standards) population, but it's huge because there is SO much that you could say about England.

It's a country that is known the world over. Go to virtually anywhere on the planet and say you're from England and they will have some idea of what you are talking about and where you are from.

England has, of course, long been a global force. Names such as Shakespeare, Queen Victoria (yes, she was a bit German), Churchill (yes, he was half-American) and Bobby Charlton are known across the world. As are Beefeaters (the folk in the fancy red costumes at the Tower of London, not the restaurant), Tower Bridge, bowler hats and gin and tonic.

This England is a special country (though, to be fair, most people in most countries think theirs is special) and so, here, in about 50,000 words, two English people (yes, we are an eighth Scottish and one of us is married to a Scot) are going to try to sum up, for anybody who is interested, what we find particularly special and/or interesting and/or amusing about this great country, this royal throne of kings (and queens), this scepter'd isle, this other Eden, demi-paradise, this England (had to go a bit Shakespearean there).

Welcome to *The Little Book of England* (which is most definitely NOT *The Book of Little England* – that would be something else entirely).

1

SO WHERE DID ENGLAND COME FROM?

Some people say, 'You only know where you're going, if you know where you're coming from.' With England, that could be a bit of a problem, since nobody really knows exactly where it came from or how it came into being.

A lot of countries have pretty much agreed origin stories. Sure, there are historical controversies and debates, but the country's people have a broad sense of what happened when and how it led to the creation of their nation.

The origins of England, however, are situated deep in what used to be known (and, by many, are still known) as the Dark Ages. This was a phrase invented to indicate the comparative lack of historical sources for the period but has the rather unfortunate effect that people somehow instinctively think the period itself was rather dark. So, in movies about the period, you tend to get a lot of people wandering around looking rather depressed under grey skies. However, there were probably many warm and sunny days during the Dark Ages (well, this is England, so perhaps not that many) and historians today tend to prefer the term 'the Early Medieval Period'. Basically, it's what happened after the end of Roman Britain.

WHAT DID THE ROMANS EVER DO HERE?

The Romans, of course, had, by AD 410, been here for some time. Julius Caesar (yes, him), having slaughtered his way across Gaul, turned up here in 55 and 54 BC and found a lot of tribes who were the result of millennia of immigration into Britain, migration within Britain and occasional peaceful co-existence and a lot of mutual slaughter.

Caesar had a lot of trouble with the weather (no surprise there then) and with some of the locals, who were generally unenthusiastic about joining the Roman world and showed their lack of enthusiasm in the traditional manner, by chucking spears at the invaders. Caesar returned to Gaul, not having achieved much, and declared victory. Well, he was writing the history of his own ventures himself, so he could do that sort of thing.

Almost a century would pass after that before another Roman leader would dare to send his troops across the Channel. To the Romans, who were very much part of a Mediterranean-based empire, Britain just seemed extremely far away and, to them, the Channel was part of Oceanus, the uncharted ocean that surrounded the known world. It all seemed pretty uninviting to Romans and Emperor Claudius only decided to invade because the Romans had already invaded everywhere else that was closer and had a better climate.

In AD 43 the legions landed in Britain again. Some of the British tribes had now decided they quite liked the idea of joining the Roman world, and assisted, or at least didn't oppose, the newcomers. A lack of British unity and a more determined display from the legions, this time, eventually produced Roman Britain.

Some Britons, such as Caratacus and Boudicca and her Iceni, were still very unenthusiastic about the whole idea, but this combination of imperial brutality and Roman cultivation of some of the British tribal leaders eventually led to Roman control across all of what is now Wales, and across England up to Hadrian's Wall.

It didn't, however, lead to huge enthusiasm for Roman culture across the whole of the island. In much of the west and north, people went on living their lives pretty much as they had before the Romans arrived. In Caledonia, the locals were particularly unenthusiastic about Rome. Every so often, the legions would advance north of Hadrian's Wall on a mission to occupy the whole of the island and, every time, after a while and defeated by a combination of the weather, the distances and locals throwing things at them, the Romans would eventually give up and retreat to Hadrian's Wall.

This turned into a bit (or actually quite a lot) of a strategic nightmare for the Roman Empire. They never managed to control the whole of Britain, and because (after all the problems they experienced in Caledonia) they didn't even seriously consider tackling Hibernia (Ireland), Roman Britain was a vulnerable little bit of the Empire, separated from mainland Europe by Oceanus and surrounded by enemies.

Consequently, the Romans had to keep a big chunk of their army here during the entire period of the Roman occupation of Britain. This produced some unexpected results of its own. The

Roman soldiers here were often bored and the Channel that separated the island from Europe made it a nice little place for rebellious generals to establish themselves before leading legions into mainland Europe to attempt to seize the imperial throne. One of these rebellions would change the history of the entire world, another would see British troops reach the Adriatic and another would destroy Roman Britain and, in the end, the whole Roman Empire too.

In AD 306, the troops of Constantine acclaimed him emperor in York. He then led his troops into mainland Europe, took Rome in AD 312, and in AD 313 began the process of making the Roman Empire officially Christian.

In AD 383, another general, Magnus Maximus, would also lead his British army into Europe. He has no link to Maximus Decimus Meridius (of *Gladiator* fame) nor, despite some of his coins carrying the legend 'MAG MAX', does he have any connection to Mad Max (of *Mad Max* fame). The venture of Magnus Maximus was not quite as successful as that of Constantine. He was defeated and executed in AD 388 in Aquileia near northern Italy's Adriatic coast, though he does still live on in Welsh medieval legend as Macsen Wledig (as in 'The Dream of Macsen Wledig').

Then, in the early fifth century, the British legions thought they'd give it another go. In AD 407 they acclaimed another bloke called Constantine as emperor, perhaps because it was almost exactly a century since the first Constantine had launched his rebellion and because it had worked so well that time. Unfortunately for Constantine III (as he is known to history) and his troops, it wasn't going to work that well this time, and the ensuing chaos was going to have huge consequences for the Roman Empire, Britain and England.

It all went quite well for him to begin with. He seized control of Gaul and made plans to take control of the rest of western Europe. However, it wasn't just Constantine's army that was on the move in Gaul. At the end of AD 406, a huge mass of people, including Vandals (that's the type with a big 'V', not the blokes with a small 'v', who break things for fun), Alans (not all of them called Alan) and Suebi (not all of them suave, though some of them may have been) had crossed the Rhine and advanced into Roman-controlled territory.

At the time, Roman commanders tended to see such groups more as potential recruits to fight in various Roman civil wars than as any big threat to the Empire and, while Constantine III and other Roman commanders were fighting each other, the Vandals, Alans and Suebi managed to make it across Gaul into Spain, where they made themselves at home and established their own kingdoms. As other groups from the east arrived within the Empire, other such kingdoms would be established and, eventually, there would be nothing much left of the western Roman Empire.

Meanwhile, in Britain, the locals had pretty much had enough. They were still paying their taxes but most of the Roman army that was supposed to be defending them from raiders attacking them from west, north and east was in mainland Europe, fighting other Romans.

Britain had never really been high on the list of imperial priorities and, at that time, with civil wars raging and a lot of blokes freshly arrived in the Empire also wandering around heavily armed and looking for plunder and land, Britain pretty much didn't figure on the list of imperial priorities at all.

In about AD 410, Britain rebelled and left the empire, and the empire hardly even noticed. By AD 411, Constantine III was dead and Britain was on its own against other bunches of heavily armed men who would soon start arriving on the island in significant numbers.

A NEW NORTH SEA FERRY SERVICE

These bunches of heavily armed men (with some women, armed or not) were coming from various directions. There were groups coming across the Irish Sea from Ireland. There were groups coming south from the lands beyond Hadrian's Wall. And there were groups coming across the North Sea and Channel.

These last groups contained a wide range of ethnic groupings, including some Franks and Frisians, but the main three groups were Angles, Saxons and Jutes. Again, there was probably some fluidity among the groups but, in brief, a lot of people from northern Germany and southern Scandinavia were looking across the North Sea and thinking that Britain looked like a good destination for building a new life (well, the weather was better here in winter). Once they got to Britain, bringing a lot of their own culture, they would establish cultural zones that sort of divide into Angles, Saxons and Jutes.

Now this is where it all gets a bit difficult to identify what exactly is happening and who is doing what to whom and with whom, which in terms of understanding England and English history is very unfortunate, since this is pretty much where England originates.

There had, of course, been people in Britain for a very long time, and there must have been still lots here when the Angles, Saxons and Jutes started arriving in significant numbers in the first half of the fifth century. There was also some fluidity in Celtic tribal identities, but the Romans had sort of cemented in place the tribal structure they encountered when they invaded the island by making the tribes the basis of their civil administration structure here.

There were Catuvellauni, Trinovantes, Iceni, Atrebates, Dobunni, Brigantes and lots of other tribes here when the Romans arrived, and there almost certainly were these same peoples still here when Roman power disappeared in AD 410. However, since the period after this sees the disappearance of a lot of the archaeologically visible culture of Roman Britain, including things such as coins, mass-produced pottery and Roman-type architecture, it's very hard to know exactly how many Britons there still were and what exactly they were up to.

The Victorians used to think this disappearance of much of the culture of Roman Britain was caused by Angles, Saxons and Jutes rampaging through villages and towns, slaughtering and burning enthusiastically. They were aided in this view by the writings of one Gildas, a British cleric writing in the early sixth century, who is pretty much our major source for the earliest decades of English history and who did indeed include some pretty gory rampaging in his account of the period. However, archaeologically, it looks likely that the main disappearance of Roman culture, in fact, mostly happened before the Angles, Saxons and Jutes arrived here in any quantity. So, people have gone looking for other possible causes.

Some have suggested climate change (in this instance, the weather getting colder rather than hotter), some have looked at the possibility of plagues, others have suggested a massive financial crisis brought on by the withdrawal of Roman government. A major possibility is that, in the power vacuum left by Rome, the tribes fought each other for control of valuable land and resources in a series of civil wars.

Most likely, there was a combination of causes, but whatever this exact combination was, the result was that the newcomers from across the North Sea were arriving in a land where the local culture and economy was considerably weakened and there was probably some land unfarmed and available.

So, what exactly happened next? The short answer is nobody really knows. We don't know how many Britons were still in the east and south of Britain when the Angles, Saxons and Jutes arrived. We don't know how many Angles, Saxons and Jutes arrived. We don't know whether the Britons mainly fought the newcomers or the newcomers mainly settled peacefully alongside the existing residents. We don't know whether the newcomers mainly intermarried with the locals, or instead mainly evicted them and sent them fleeing westwards. In short, we don't really know whether early England was mainly an Anglo-Saxon country or mainly a British Celtic country with an Anglo-Saxon veneer, in which many Britons adopted Anglo-Saxon culture, just as many of them had previously adopted Roman culture.

Efforts have been made, using DNA analysis, to try to work out what proportion of the population's DNA in early England had origins on the other side of the North Sea, and what proportion had British origins, but the results suggested by different analyses have varied widely. What can be said with some certainty is that (not surprisingly) the highest proportion of newcomer DNA is found in places closest to mainland Europe, such as East Anglia, while in western parts of England, several DNA groupings seem to have been there since the Iron Age and seem probably to represent the tribes that the Romans found in Britain when they arrived here.

So, now we come to the historical record, such as it is. This has been assembled from three main sources, Gildas, the British cleric writing in the early sixth century, already mentioned, Bede (yes, the Venerable) an Anglo-Saxon monk writing mainly in the early eighth century, and the *Anglo-Saxon Chronicle*, first assembled perhaps in the ninth century. You'll notice from the dates that none of this is exactly what you'd call contemporary reporting of what went on in fifth-century Britain, but from the various sources it is possible to assemble a rough kind of narrative for what was perhaps going on in some places at that time.

We have already seen how Roman commanders in mainland Europe unintentionally allowed newcomers to establish kingdoms within their borders. Something similar seems to have happened in at least one instance here. A British ruler, perhaps called Vortigern, allowed Saxons to settle within his realm in about AD 449, on the understanding they would fight for him against his enemies. However, a pay dispute happened and, instead of just going on strike or going to arbitration, the Saxons, perhaps led by two characters, Hengist and Horsa, decided that they would like their own kingdom in Britain instead. After a certain amount of slaughtering, they got that, establishing the kingdom of Kent.

The new kingdom took its name from the existing British tribe in the area, the Cantii, and some of its early warriors seem to have worn metalwork which incorporated Roman and British design elements but, nonetheless, there was a new power in the land.

In 1949, a boat (somewhat confusingly a replica Viking, not Saxon, boat) was sailed from Denmark to Kent to mark the 1,500th anniversary of Hengist and Horsa's supposed arrival. And today, the Hugin replica is on display at Pegwell Bay in Kent.

A LOT OF KINGS AND KINGDOMS

Over the next century and a half, more such kingdoms emerged, accompanied with, again, some more slaughtering. These included the South Saxons (a name that would become Sussex) and the West Saxons (a name that would become Wessex). There were also the East Saxons (yep, Essex) and the Middle Saxons

(Middlesex). The last lot never really made it as a kingdom but would later (much later) do quite well with cricket.

But what of those Angles, I hear you say? Well, there were, of course, the East Angles (in East Anglia obviously) and the Middle Angles (who, like the Middle Saxons, never really made it as a separate kingdom), and to the north of them, the small kingdom of Lindsey (at that stage a kingdom, not a person), and then Deira and Bernicia. Deira and Bernicia were north of the Humber and would eventually become, yes, Northumbria.

And the Jutes? Well, the Jutes don't appear to have made it big over here. Kent was sort of Jutish – oh, and the Isle of Wight, and the bit of land opposite the Isle of Wight.

How Anglo-Saxon these 'Anglo-Saxon' kingdoms were is a bit unclear. Some of the kingdoms, such as Kent, had British names and the names of Lindsey, Deira and Bernicia all had British origins. And the 'Saxon' who is said to have founded Wessex, he had a British name too – Cerdic, a form of Caradoc or Caratacus.

It's all very confusing and it's hard to know exactly what was happening. Nevertheless, some kind of distinction had emerged between kingdoms in the east and south of Britain that were culturally Anglo-Saxon and generally pagan, and kingdoms in the west of Britain that were culturally British and Christian.

And there were battles between the Britons and the Anglo-Saxons, some of which the Britons won. Gildas mentions a man called Ambrosius Aurelianus, who led the Britons to victory over the Saxons, and he mentions the British victory at the siege of Mount Badon.

Having mentioned Badon, it seems a good place here to mention a name linked to Badon, Arthur. Yes, it's King Arthur himself, legend of book, stage, screen and possibly history. Arthur, if he existed, was a war commander leading Britons against the Anglo-Saxons, sometime either in the late fifth or early sixth century, yet, despite some uncertainty over his existence, he would become a hugely significant figure in the later culture both of England and Britain, as a prime example of the warrior king.

Geoffrey of Monmouth's twelfth-century work, the *History of the Kings of Britain*, which was, in fact, in large part a work of historical fiction, told Arthur's story in great detail and became a massive bestseller across England and Europe – to the extent that you could have a massive bestseller in the days when books had to be copied by hand. Two hundred manuscripts of the book remain, and that's a lot of hard work, hand-copying, by anybody's standards.

In 1191, Abbot Sully even found what was claimed to be the grave of Arthur and Guinevere in Glastonbury Abbey. It was a convenient find since the abbey had recently suffered a devastating fire and an increase in the tourist trade would help the abbey's finances. Glastonbury, of course, still gets a lot of visitors today, even if not all of them are there for King Arthur. Yes, the younger generation probably associate Glastonbury more with the festival there, rather than a post-Roman warrior who may or may not have existed and may or may not have been buried there.

Henry VII called his son and (at that stage) heir Arthur. However, the prince died young and instead of a second King Arthur, we got Henry VIII. More about him later in the book.

And Arthur kept on inspiring writers over the centuries. In the fifteenth century, for instance, there was Sir Thomas Malory's *Le Morte d'Arthur*. In the nineteenth century came Tennyson's 'Idylls of the King'. In the twentieth century, we had assorted Arthur movies, and yes, of course, *Monty Python and the Holy Grail*, and its musical, *Spamalot*.

However, we now need to return to the sixth century, where Gildas was being somewhat less than inspired by Constantine, King of Dumnonia (Devon, Cornwall and a bit of Somerset). Tintagel, in Cornwall, the reputed birthplace of Arthur, was almost certainly one of his strongholds, but Gildas did not see Constantine as a noble warrior king. Constantine's sins, according to Gildas, included multiple adulteries and attacking two royal youths at a church altar. He was never going to get nominated for Pious King of the Year.

Gildas was none too keen on some of the British royals but, there again, he didn't like the pagan Saxons either. Gildas is said to have died in about 570 and he really wouldn't have liked what was about to come next.

In 577, at the Battle of Deorham (now Dyrham near Bath), a West Saxon force under Ceawlin (another British name, basically, Colin) and his son Cuthwine defeated a British army, killed three British kings and captured Gloucester, Cirencester and Bath. With this battle, the Anglo-Saxons destroyed the last remaining British kingdom (probably the successor to the mighty Dobunni tribe) in what is now south-central England, and reached the western sea, cutting the land route between the Britons in Cornwall and Devon and the Britons in what is now Wales. Just a few years later, in the early 600s, a Northumbrian force under King Æthelfrith destroyed another British army in a battle at Chester, threatening the land route between Wales and the Britons to the north in Cumbria (a name that has the same origins as Cymru, the Welsh word for Wales) and beyond.

Gildas would, however, have approved of some developments in the Anglo-Saxon kingdoms in the decades after his death, because Christianity was coming to the Anglo-Saxons. It all perhaps started in a slightly questionable fashion. Pope Gregory allegedly saw some blond boys in a slave market in Rome, asked who they were and, on being told they were Angles, made some quip about them being more angels than Angles. Presumably Gregory liked (at least some of) his angels to be blonde.

Anyway, allegedly on the basis of all that, Gregory in Rome decided that he would reach out across Oceanus to this land. He assembled a task force of about forty, under a priest called Augustine, and despatched it to England. Soon after that, however, he had to despatch them again to England, because Augustine had returned with a plea not to be sent to this distant island lurking on the edge of the known world.

In 597, Augustine finally landed, like the legions before him, in Kent. He was, however, on a peaceful mission and, fortunately for him, unlike what had happened to the legions, none of the locals threw anything sharp at him. Soon, with the permission of King Æthelbert of Kent, and the encouragement of his Frankish and Christian wife, Bertha, Augustine and his mission had established themselves in the capital of Kent, Canterbury. The Archbishop of Canterbury is, of course, the head of the Church of England today.

ONE BIG KINGDOM

Christianity would spread fairly fast through the Anglo-Saxon kingdoms in the seventh century. Meanwhile, the kings of the various Anglo-Saxons were competing enthusiastically for political and military power. The Anglo-Saxons were still occasionally advancing against the Britons in the west, but they were also spending a lot of time fighting each other and trying to acquire dominance over each other. This was, as yet, nothing resembling an actual Kingdom of England, but, somewhere amidst all the fighting, there did develop the concept of the Bretwalda.

We have already seen how hard it is to know what was going on in this whole period, so it won't surprise you that people can't entirely agree on what the word 'Bretwalda' means. It might mean 'ruler of Britain' or, it might mean 'ruler of a wide domain'. Broadly speaking, however, it does seem to have been a term that was applied to the king in each generation who was the pre-eminent king in England – the king who had power and influence over the other kings and princes. It was probably not an official title, but more a matter of opinion and an acknowledgment of the realities of power in an England where, ultimately, power came from the sword's sharp edge. Bede gives a list of pre-eminent kings, which includes Ceawlin of

Wessex – the bloke who, among other conquests, captured Bath, Gloucester and Cirencester – and Æthelbert of Kent.

After Æthelbert, he goes on to Rædwald of East Anglia. Now, since this is the king who was probably buried with the sumptuous Sutton Hoo treasure, it does indeed seem reasonable to see him as a king who may have had some kind of special status among other kings.

Interestingly, although generally the Sutton Hoo treasure is regarded as a superb example of Anglo-Saxon taste and craftsmanship (which generally it is), there are pieces in it that are (or may be) of British manufacture. There is, for instance, a spectacular British hanging bowl and it has been argued that a magnificent, large ceremonial whetstone, kitted out as a sceptre, is also of British manufacture.

After Rædwald, Bede continues with his list to a bunch of north-eastern kings. These were powerful people and, since Bede himself lived and worked in the north-east, it was also, no doubt, useful for him to compliment local royalty. In doing so, however, Bede ignores a figure who should feature in such a list of pre-eminent kings – one of the most interesting and enigmatic characters of early British and English history, Penda of Mercia.

Penda was a pagan, which is almost certainly one reason why the Venerable (and very Christian) Bede didn't want him in his list. Another reason was that Penda spent quite a lot of his time invading the north-east, which was Bede's home territory.

The origins of Penda are unknown and there may have been Britons in his family as well as Anglo-Saxons. It is clear, however, that Penda created Mercia as one of the great kingdoms of Anglo-Saxon England, dominating the centre of Britain and spreading its power in all directions. Interestingly, while other Anglo-Saxon kings were attacking the Britons, Penda allied himself with Britons to attack Anglo-Saxons.

In 633, for instance, with Cadwallon, King of Gwynedd, he defeated and killed Edwin of Northumbria (one of Bede's list of pre-eminent kings) at the Battle of Hatfield Chase, fought most probably near Doncaster. The amazing Staffordshire Hoard is connected to the early history of Mercia. The close alliance between Mercia and Welsh kings would not last, but Mercia itself (the name probably means something like 'Land of the borders') would go on to play a huge role in English history. And the name is still used today – as in the British Army's Mercian Regiment or the West Mercia Police.

Despite some of his biases, Bede is, of course, a huge figure in English literature and in the writing of English history. And it is possible to see in him how the idea of a broader identity, which encompassed peoples from various Anglo-Saxon kingdoms, was beginning to emerge when he was writing in the early eighth century. His most famous work, for instance, is called in Latin the *Historia Ecclesiastica Gentis Anglorum*, but is known in English as the *Ecclesiastical History of the English People*. Sometime around 900, one of Bede's Latin references to English territory was translated into English as '*Engla londe*', a term that would eventually become '*Englaland*' and then, yes, England.

Mercia continued to do well for itself during the eighth century, with the so-called Mercian Supremacy (a lot more swords than in the *Bourne Supremacy*). This was the age of King Offa of Mercia, whose name is now attached to the mighty Offa's Dyke earthwork in the Welsh borders.

However, the power of Wessex was starting to rise, a process that was somewhat abruptly interrupted by the arrival of, yes, the Vikings. And no, they didn't have horns or wings on their helmets. It would have been fairly impractical in battle, even if such helmets do look rather fun in Victorian illustrations.

The Vikings arrived originally as raiders but soon saw an opportunity to take land permanently in a country that had, again, rather warmer winters than their own. The Vikings had conquered huge amounts of England when Alfred (the Great, of course) managed to inflict a decisive defeat on them at the Battle of Edington in 878.

Wessex was taking control. Alfred died in 899, but his son Edward the Elder continued the process, ending up controlling perhaps most of England, in fact, and because of that he took the title 'King of the Anglo-Saxons'. His son, Æthelstan, continued the process and took the titles 'King of the Whole of Britain', which he wasn't, and 'King of the English', which he pretty much was.

Edgar, who ruled from 959 to 975, consolidated the English kingdom, and England had pretty much arrived as a country. Obviously, there would be changes of ruler and changes of dynasty, and eventually England would be linked to the other constituent parts of what is now the United Kingdom of Great Britain and Northern Ireland, but from about the tenth and eleventh centuries we can say that there is a place called England.

So, what is this England and who are the people who have lived in it and who live in it now? In the rest of this little book, we are going to take a little look.

2

A LOT OF KINGS, QUEENS, PRINCES, PRINCESSES ... AND SOME PRIME MINISTERS

In 2022, Queen Elizabeth II passed away. She was, as is well known, the longest-reigning British monarch, having reigned for seventy years and reaching her Platinum Jubilee. Her great-great-grandmother, Queen Victoria, was, by comparison, just a novice when she died, having reigned from 1837 to 1901, a mere sixty-three-and-a-bit years.

Elizabeth II was, of course, the Queen of the United Kingdom of Great Britain and Northern Ireland, but she came from a long line of royals stretching back to kings and queens of England and, of course, Scotland, and, considering how interconnected the royal houses of Europe are, quite a lot of other places.

What makes England England is, of course, primarily its people, land and cultures, and we'll come onto those in the meat of the book, but if you ask people around the world to think of something connected with England and its culture and history, a lot of them will mention a royal or two, so it's worth now taking a brief saunter through the line-up.

EARLY ROYALS

There have been royals in what is now England for a VERY long time, since well before the Romans, in fact. We have already mentioned Caratacus, who was here when the Romans turned up in AD 43, and coins produced in the last century before Roman rule carry several legends, most of which are almost certainly the names of rulers. There is, for instance, BODVOC of the Dobunni tribe (not linked to Badvoc, a main character of 1980s/1990s Roman-British sitcom, *Chelmsford 123*), based in Gloucestershire and surrounding areas. There is COMMIOS of the Atrebates, near the south coast, and CVNOBELINUS of the Catuvellauni-Trinovantes in the Hertfordshire/Bedfordshire/Essex sort of area, a king who had a bit of a second career 1,600 years later as the main character in Shakespeare's play, *Cymbeline*.

We have already mentioned a lot of the kings of the period between the end of Roman Britain and the arrival of the Normans, and it's worth mentioning here a few of the queens as well. Æthelflæd, daughter of Alfred the Great, for example, ruled Mercia alone, after the death of her husband, as Lady of the Mercians. A formidable woman, she extended Mercia's defence against the Vikings and then went on the offensive against them, capturing Derby and Leicester and threatening York.

And what about Ælfthryth? She was the first queen consort who was actually crowned. She was also the stepmother of King Edward the Martyr, who died somewhat mysteriously at Corfe Castle, or thereabouts, leaving the throne vacant for Ælfthryth's son, Æthelred. This is, of course, the Æthelred who was famously, or infamously, Unready. It's not quite as it sounds, though, since Unready didn't mean he was late for meetings or something. The original Anglo-Saxon word meant he was poorly advised – although perhaps he was late for some meetings as well.

There is also seventh-century Balthild, who seems to have been Anglo-Saxon by birth but ended up as queen to Frankish King Clovis II and, after his death, as powerful queen regent. Fascinatingly, a gold seal matrix marked on one side 'BALDAHILDIS' in Frankish lettering and with a woman's face was found in Norfolk in 1999. And the fascination doesn't end there because on the other side of the matrix is shown a naked couple getting very friendly.

Apart from poor old Edward, it's also worth mentioning a couple of royal martyrs who ended up saints as well as kings. Statistically, as a monarch, you were much more likely to die violently in medieval England than in modern England, but there again, statistically, you were much more likely to end up as a saint as well.

Oswald of Northumbria died fighting against pagan Penda of Mercia at the Battle of Maserfield in 642 and, soon after his death, was acclaimed a saint. There are a still several churches dedicated to St Oswald today. In the ninth century, Edmund, King of East Anglia, tried to defend his kingdom against marauding Vikings and instead ended up dead in 869. He was then made a saint with a shrine at, yes, Bury St Edmunds. St Edmund's body was indeed buried at some stage at Bury St Edmunds but, somewhat confusingly, the Bury in Bury St Edmunds is from the Anglo-Saxon word '*burg*', for town.

It took a long time for England's royals to end the Viking threat. A lot of Vikings would settle in England and their families would eventually become peaceful and productive members of English society, but there was a LOT of fighting first.

Despite all the successes of Alfred the Great and his kids against the Vikings, there would be still more of the Scandinavians heading across the North Sea to England before it all ended. Æthelred the Unready didn't have a great time trying to counter them, and his son Edmund Ironside (despite having a rather sexier nickname – no link, incidentally, to the San Francisco TV detective of that name) wasn't entirely successful either.

Soon Danish Canute, or Cnut, was on the throne. Yes, it's that bloke sitting on his throne on the beach ordering the sea not to get his feet wet and being ignored by the sea. To be fair, it seems likely that if this ever happened, he was probably demonstrating that even the mightiest humans don't control the forces of nature and, to be fair again, it may not have happened, since it's first mentioned by a bloke writing in the early twelfth century, about 100 years after the supposed event.

The English managed to see off Canute/Cnut's successors, and when another Viking army arrived in the north in 1066, it was decisively defeated at the Battle of Stamford Bridge (nothing to do with the Chelsea ground), near York. However, if the English thought they were now safe from Viking armies arriving uninvited, they were reckoning without a bunch who had, some time before, settled in northern France, just across the Channel from England, and somewhat unsportingly disguised themselves as French, slightly changing their name from Norsemen to Normans.

IT'S THOSE NORMANS!

Yes, it's William the Conqueror with the Battle of Hastings (which wasn't actually at Hastings but was at Battle) in 1066 and all the rest of it, with Harold definitely dead, and possibly killed by an arrow in the face.

Pretty much everyone has heard of the Battle of Hastings, but that wasn't the end of it. The capture of England by William and his Normans was messy and often brutal. English rebellions against his rule took place for some time, and his so-called Harrying of the North was an appalling rampage of destruction, looting and slaughter that has few parallels in the history of England.

There is a tendency to think that the Norman royals marked a totally new dynasty in England with no link to the Anglo-Saxon royals, but there is a link, and she is known to history as Matilda of Scotland. Matilda was the daughter of Margaret of Wessex who, in turn, was granddaughter of Edmund Ironside and the wife of the Scottish king, Malcolm III.

Matilda was educated at Romsey Abbey in Hampshire and then Wilton Abbey in Wiltshire, and when Henry I, William's son, was looking for a bride, he chose Matilda, giving himself and his heirs greater legitimacy in English eyes due to her descent from Anglo-Saxon kings. When Henry was away fighting (which he often was), she would act as regent.

She and Henry had a daughter who was, yes, the now rather more widely known Matilda of medieval Britain, the Empress Matilda, England's only empress until the era of the British Empire. Not that she was Empress of England, as such. She was empress because in 1114 she married, in Germany, the Holy Roman Emperor Henry V, who was much older than her and died not that long afterwards.

In 1135, her father Henry died and there was a succession crisis in England. Matilda's cousin Stephen seized the throne. Matilda wasn't having any of it, and invaded England. A vicious civil war ensued which has become known as The Anarchy (anarchy in England but, apart from that, not much link to 'Anarchy in the UK' by the Sex Pistols). Matilda failed to take the throne herself, but in the end, when Stephen died, her son Henry II did.

A LOT OF PEOPLE FIGHTING A LOT OF OTHER PEOPLE A LOT

The medieval period was quite violent in England. And in loads of other places.

Henry II spent a lot of time fighting in France, where he picked up a lot of land and a wife, Eleanor of Aquitaine. If he enters public awareness much these days, though, it tends to be because of four of his knights brutally slaughtering Thomas Becket, Archbishop of Canterbury, and because of his sons, two of England's best-known kings.

Yes, it's the brothers Richard I, 'the Lionheart', and John, who didn't get such a flattering nickname. Indeed, he seems to have made his own real name so unpopular in royal circles that there has never been a John II in this country.

Richard, of course, spent a lot of time slaughtering people on Crusade and in France and, in fact, despite being King of England, spent very little time actually in England. Even his wedding took place in Cyprus. And while English people getting married on Mediterranean islands is a fairly regular event these days, it was pretty unusual then.

John, by contrast, spent a lot more time in England, doing a bit of planning and rebelling in Richard's absence and eventually, when Richard died, he became king. Even though there have been recent attempts to rehabilitate John's reputation somewhat, it was not what you'd call a happy reign.

He lost loads of land in France and ended up in a huge civil war against a lot of barons. Magna Carta did at least come out of all that. Plus, there was Robin Hood – perhaps. An outlaw Robin Hood who fought the forces of King John and stole from the rich to give to the poor may never have existed, but it's a great story – even if some of the movies have been a bit questionable.

However, the country was in such a state by the time John died that there was also a French King of England alongside him. Well, sort of.

Louis VIII of France, with the help of some of the rebellious barons, invaded England in 1216 and had himself proclaimed in London as King Louis. He never managed to get himself actually crowned, and generally he doesn't appear in lists of kings of England.

It was John's son, Henry III, who managed to prevent Louis settling himself on the throne of England. Henry had a long time on the throne, a whole fifty-six years, but his reign saw vicious persecution of the Jewish community and yet another war with the barons.

Henry III was a big fan of Edward the Confessor, in religious terms, and he named his heir Edward, which at the time in royal circles was an unusual, Anglo-Saxon name. And not only was Henry III's successor an Edward, so were the next two occupants of the throne after that. So, you get, Edward I, II and III, one after the other, which is handily pretty easy to remember if you are doing a list of the monarchs of England.

Edward I spent a lot of time fighting in Wales and Scotland, where he encountered William Wallace (yes, it's Braveheart!). Edward II spent a lot of time with Piers Gaveston, who may, or may not, have been his lover, and also spent time losing to Robert the Bruce at Bannockburn and fighting the barons (again). He was forced off the throne in 1327 and probably murdered.

Edward III spent a lot of time fighting in France, sometimes very successfully, particularly at the famous Battle of Crécy in 1346 and the slightly less famous Battle of Poitiers in 1356. There would then have been an Edward IV, since Edward III's eldest son was called, yep, Edward. However, that Edward died before his father, so it was his grandson, Richard (the family seem to have decided there were enough Edwards around), who took the throne as Richard II.

Richard gained himself a reputation as a patron of the arts but found maintaining long-term stable control of the country a problem and, in the end, in 1399 his cousin Henry kicked him off the throne and Richard died in captivity. Henry became Henry IV and, son of the Duke of Lancaster as he was, ushered in the era of the House of Lancaster. You can probably see where this is going now. The Wars of the Roses are not far off.

Before that, though, we have to mention Henry V. Yes, it's Agincourt 1415, and 'once more unto the breeches', sorry, 'once more unto the breach', etc. Agincourt is generally known to the public as England's greatest victory over the French until the days of Napoleon and Waterloo (not just an English victory, that, but one involving lots of other Brits, plus Prussians, etc.).

It was, indeed, a significant victory at the time and led to a peace deal signed at Troyes in 1420, which recognised King Henry V of England as the heir to King Charles VI of France. Soon after that, Henry married Catherine of Valois, the daughter of the French king. Everything looked set for the same English royal dynasty to rule both England and France. However, soon after all that, the situation changed radically and, in terms of English ambitions, not for the better. Very definitely not for the better.

In 1422, Henry suddenly died of disease. And soon after that, Charles VI died as well. The infant son of Henry V and Catherine of Valois, Henry VI, inherited the English throne, while in France, Charles VII (the son of Charles VI, who had been shoved to one side in 1420 to make Henry V the French heir) reasserted his claim to the French throne.

A series of disasters for England followed in France (with a certain Joan of Arc playing a significant role) and in 1453 a decisive English defeat at the Battle of Castillon pretty much ended the Hundred Years War and the English empire in France. But the English royals would soon have a few other matters to worry about because in England, very soon, the Wars of the Roses started.

The Wars of the Roses almost sounds like some innocent garden dispute. It was, instead, as civil wars so often are, bitter, brutal, long and complex, with a lot of people slaughtered. And it wasn't even that connected with roses. Roses were among a variety of symbols worn by supporters and fighters of assorted factions to show their loyalty and, in battles, to prevent allies and comrades slaughtering them by mistake. But in history, it is often useful to have an agreed, widely used name for incidents and events, and these wars have become known as the Wars of the Roses, after the red rose that became associated with the House of Lancaster and the white rose that became associated with the House of York.

Basically, this was a battle for power between two dynasties with rival claims to the throne of England. The House of Lancaster set off with some serious advantages and some serious disadvantages. Its main advantage was that Henry VI, of the House of Lancaster, was on the throne. Its main disadvantage was also Henry VI, in the sense that Henry went from being an ineffective child monarch, to being an ineffective adult monarch. Often the real Lancastrian power was Henry's wife, the formidable Margaret of Anjou, niece of the King of France.

This led to rival claimants to the throne taking an interest in replacing Henry. In particular, there was Richard, Duke of York, who also had Edward III as an ancestor. Richard and Margaret competed for power over Henry VI and the English throne. In the end, in 1455, Richard, feeling his position under serious threat, led an army south. Henry's army met them at St Albans and was decisively defeated.

There would follow thirty years of intermittent fighting and plotting, as first one faction and then the other took power. In 1460, for instance, Richard of York was killed. But then in 1461, Richard's son, Edward, defeated a Lancastrian army at the Battle of Towton, where there was a particularly big death toll, with thousands dead. Edward was subsequently crowned as Edward IV, the first Yorkist king, but would then be forced into exile.

In 1471, after Yorkist victories at Barnet and then Tewkesbury, Edward was again fairly secure on the throne and, while imprisoned, Henry mysteriously died, making Edward's position even more secure. An imprisoned Margaret would be ransomed by the French in 1475 and would head south across the Channel.

In 1483, though, Edward IV died. Edward's two sons, the so-called Princes in the Tower, mysteriously disappeared and Edward's brother had himself crowned Richard III. Yes, it's the bloke from the car park in Leicester.

In 1485, Henry Tudor, a new claimant to the throne, who was connected via his mother Lady Margaret Beaufort to Edward III, landed in Wales and advanced westwards. His forces met those of Richard III at the Battle of Bosworth and Henry ended up on the throne of England as Henry VII, while Richard ended up buried in what was then Greyfriars Church in Leicester but was, by 2012 when they dug him up, a car park. Richard's bones have now been reburied in a rather more dignified location, Leicester Cathedral.

THOSE TUDOR TIMES

And so we come to the Tudors, perhaps England's most widely known royal dynasty. Henry VII was quite a careful ruler, attempting to establish his new dynasty firmly and stabilise the country after the chaos of the Wars of the Roses. He married Elizabeth of York, the daughter of Edward IV, to reinforce his claim to the throne and he introduced the so-called Tudor rose as a symbol that combined the white rose of York with the red rose of Lancaster.

Henry VII's son and heir, Henry VIII, was, by contrast, as is pretty well known, a very different kind of character. To be fair to Henry, he wasn't initially supposed to be Henry VII's heir. As mentioned earlier, Henry VII's eldest son and the intended successor was Prince Arthur.

The future Henry VIII was 10 when his elder brother died and he suddenly found himself thrust into the position of heir to the throne. It is also worth considering that when Henry was born, in 1491, it was only six years after the Battle of Bosworth, which put his father, somewhat unexpectedly to many, on the throne. The future Henry VIII grew up in a very uncertain world where the Tudor dynasty had yet to establish deep roots, and where he knew from recent history how a weak dynasty or a dynasty with a disputed succession could quickly become prey to rival claimants to the throne.

All of this, to some extent, explains Henry VIII's worries about security and his desperate search for a son, but does not justify Henry's cruelty to some of those around him. The young, athletic, good-looking Henry eventually became the fat, old debauched Henry known from the portraits. His search for a new wife, one who would give him a male heir, led to the split with the Roman Catholic Church and the creation of the Church of England. He spent vast amounts of money on himself and his projects, including various unsuccessful military adventures. He did, however, help to create the English navy. When he died in 1547, Henry VIII left a dynasty in trouble.

Henry's successor, Edward VI, was just 9 years old when he was suddenly put on the throne. Edward himself would die in 1553, when he was just 15. A regency council ruled for him during his brief reign. Edward named as his successor Lady Jane Grey (yes, her), his first cousin once removed, who happened to be married to the son of John Dudley, Duke of Northumberland, who happened to be running the regency council in the later years of Edward's life.

Edward VI was also a huge supporter of the Church of England, as was Lady Jane Grey. The other main competitor for the throne, Mary, Henry VIII's eldest daughter, was a Catholic. Jane is sometimes known as the Nine Days' Queen, because that's pretty much all the time there was between her being proclaimed queen and the Privy Council of England deciding they'd go for Mary instead. Jane was later executed during Mary's reign.

It would be hard to see Mary's time on the throne as a huge success. Henry's creation of the Church of England had involved a lot of disruption. Mary's attempt to make England a Catholic country again also involved a lot of disruption. Her marriage to Philip II (the same bloke who would later send the Spanish Armada against Elizabethan England) was hugely controversial and did not produce a child. When Mary died in 1558 after a brief reign, her sister, the last Tudor monarch, found herself on the throne.

Elizabeth I is another of those English monarchs who, like Henry VIII, is instantly recognisable to a lot of people. She was queen from 1558 to 1603 and her reign saw the Spanish Armada, English explorations (and privateering, sort of officially sanctioned piracy) around the globe, the beginnings of an English empire, Francis Drake, Sir Walter Raleigh, the beginning of Shakespeare's career and so on. She was, by the low standards set by monarchs like her father, cautious, careful and effective. Many of her subjects even liked her. She acquired nicknames such as Gloriana and Good Queen Bess.

Yet, as with Henry VIII, Edward VI and Mary before her, she failed to establish a succession that would leave the Tudor dynasty stable and unquestioned. She never married, never produced an heir, and there was the whole matter of Mary, Queen of Scots, who had her own claim to the English throne. In the end, Elizabeth had Mary executed in 1586 but, when Elizabeth died in 1603, it was Mary's son, James VI of Scotland, who became James I of England, uniting the royal houses of the two kingdoms.

STUARTS, A BUNCH OF GEORGES AND THE LOT WHO CAME AFTER THEM

James has only really made it into today's public consciousness because of the Gunpowder Plot and the famous translation into English of the Bible – the *Authorized King James* version. He was also the father of Charles I, who is widely known for a whole lot of other reasons, and mainly for having his head cut off by his own people.

Yes, it's the English Civil War! Although, these days, historians tend to recognise that it wasn't actually that English since it was also linked to a lot of fighting that included other places and other nationalities, particularly Scotland and the Scottish, and Ireland and the Irish.

Like Henry VIII, Charles was not initially supposed to be king. But when, in 1612, his elder brother Henry Frederick died, Charles was thrust into the role of heir. In 1625, he married Henrietta Maria of France and in 1626, when James died, he became king. By 1642, people had started slaughtering each other in a civil war between the forces of Parliament and the forces of the king.

Charles was inflexible, authoritarian and made some very unwise decisions. In an earlier time, he might have got away with all that, but by the time of his reign, Parliament had become much more assertive and was also suspicious of Henrietta Maria's Catholicism and the king's attitude to the Church of England.

Parliament found effective military leadership in figures like Oliver Cromwell. After the war and a lot of plotting, Charles was convicted in 1649 of treason against his country and was executed soon after. There then followed a period when England had no monarch. It is called the Commonwealth and has basically nothing whatsoever to do with today's Commonwealth, which consists of nations that were, mostly, once part of the British Empire.

Oliver Cromwell was Lord Protector and the chief figure in the Commonwealth. However, his death in 1658 led to yet another succession crisis and the son of Charles I, Charles II, ended up back on the throne.

Under Charles II, England made great advances in the cultural and scientific areas. There were also the great disasters of 1665, the Great Plague of London, and 1666, the Great Fire of London – not great years to be a Londoner really. Charles had sex with a LOT of women and fathered a lot of children. However, his marriage to Catherine of Braganza produced no heir and when Charles died in 1685, his death produced instead yet another royal succession crisis.

His heir, his brother James, was Catholic. In 1688, James and his wife had a son. Key members of the political establishment decided to get rid of James before he could re-establish a Catholic monarchy in England. Across from the Netherlands came William of Orange with his wife, Mary, who happened to be the daughter of James II, but who also happened to have been raised as an Anglican.

James fled to France (family dinners involving him and his daughter would have been pretty awkward after the rebellion anyway) and William and Mary reigned jointly as, well, William and Mary. That is, they did until Mary died and then William reigned alone and was succeeded in 1702 by Mary's sister, Anne.

Queen Anne now seems to be largely known as a furniture type and a leading character in the recent movie, *The Favourite*. Anne's death in 1714 led to, yes, you guessed it, yet another succession crisis.

The Catholic family of James II were still around in mainland Europe, but, instead of them, Anne's second cousin George, Elector of Hanover, ended up on the throne. He would be followed by George I, George II (in 1745, Bonnie Prince Charlie tried and failed to kick him off the throne), George III (who lost America and had some very serious mental health problems) and George IV (Prince Regent during the period when his father was unable to rule, and then king himself). This, like Edward I, II and III getting on the throne in order, is nice and easy to remember.

We have been looking at the royals in this chapter because, for much of England's history, the monarchs, due to their unique role in governing the country, pretty much defined their era. The time of Edward II, for instance, was VERY different to the time of Charles II. However, somewhere along the line it became the prime minister and occupant of 10 Downing Street who would become the real power in government and who would define what England (and Britain) became.

So, this being the *LITTLE Book of England*, where we don't have space to mention everything, we will now just quickly run through the monarchs after the Georgian period, before returning to take a look through some of the more interesting PMs there have been.

William IV, younger brother of George IV ruled from 1830 to 1837, and is notable because he wasn't yet another George. But then, with his elder brother already being George, that could have got really confusing when they were growing up. He was succeeded by his niece Victoria.

Yes, it's Queen Victoria herself. Somehow, one feels, Queen Victoria was much more a British and global figure rather than specifically English. She is, after all, known for her love of Scotland, for being married to the German Prince Albert, for being connected to most of the royal houses of Europe and being called, therefore, 'the grandmother of Europe', and for ruling much of the world. Nowadays, of course, she is known as the pub in *Eastenders*.

After Victoria, came Edward VII, who had a lot of mistresses. Then it was another George V, who was king during the First World War, when Britain and the Empire fought his cousin, Kaiser Wilhelm II. George V had a beard and big moustache, Kaiser Wilhelm just had a big moustache.

When George V died in 1936, there was yet another succession crisis. This was the one involving Edward VIII and Mrs Simpson. After Edward abdicated, his younger brother took over, as George VI. He, of course, was the father of Queen Elizabeth II and the grandfather of King Charles III.

AND THOSE PRIME MINISTERS AT LAST!

Monarchs have, of course, had ministers, in the sense of people they trust to go out there and get done what they want done, pretty much since monarchs started being monarchs. Being minister to a monarch was often both a high-potential reward and a high-potential risk kind of job. When the most powerful person in the country trusted you with running the country, you could easily end up very rich or very executed, or first very rich and then very executed. It can be tough being the occupant of 10 Downing Street today, but at least prime ministers don't get sentenced to death when their popularity ends.

Sometimes, ministers could be chosen just because the monarch enjoyed spending time with them but, generally, for obvious reasons, the monarch wanted somebody who could, at the very least, read, write and understand numbers. For this reason, during the Middle Ages when such qualities were rather rare, the Crown's chief minister was often a minister of the religious type as well.

The unfortunate Archbishop Thomas Becket was Henry II's Lord Chancellor before the knights turned up to express Henry's displeasure by slaughtering him. And, of course, Henry VIII, a monarch who relied heavily on chief ministers to allow him more time for carousing, hunting, pursuing mistresses and desperately searching for an heir had, at one stage, Cardinal Wolsey, as his Lord Chancellor and chief fixer. When Wolsey fell out of favour during the crisis over already married Henry's attempts to marry Anne Boleyn, the cardinal was charged with treason but died before a trial.

Next up as Henry's chief minister was Sir Thomas More. After three years, Henry charged him with treason, and this time the minister was executed.

Then it was the turn of Thomas Cromwell. He lasted eight years before being charged with treason and executed.

Elizabeth I relied heavily for much of her reign on William Cecil. He wasn't charged with treason and wasn't executed.

The Stuarts made some interesting choices of advisers and ministers. James I, for instance, had George Villiers, Duke of Buckingham, who was a close, personal friend of the king and was possibly his lover. Villiers was murdered three years after the death of James.

Charles I had, among other advisers and ministers, Thomas Wentworth, the Earl of Strafford, who was executed in 1641. Unlike Henry VIII's executed chief ministers, though, Strafford mainly died because he had fallen out with Parliament. Parliament had been around since the thirteenth century and its power had gradually grown. As with so much about life generally, much of the expansion of Parliament's authority was to do with control of the purse strings. It became accepted that, if the monarch wanted money from taxes, then he had to get Parliament's agreement, and since monarchs did indeed want money (feasting, building palaces and cathedrals and, in particular, fighting wars are all hugely expensive), they had to deal with Parliament.

In the seventeenth century the idea developed that, actually, Parliament, as the representative of England's people, had as much or more right to direct the daily running of the country than did the monarch. In 1649, instead of Henry VIII executing a chief minister for treason because the king decided his minister had let him down, Parliament executed a monarch for treason because it decided the king had let the country down.

The monarchy was restored in 1660, but the message of 1649 was not lost on subsequent monarchs. In 1707, the United Kingdom was formed from the crowns of England and Scotland, and in the eighteenth century the principle became established that the monarch's prime minister was a person who could control Parliament, which is pretty much the state still today.

Robert Walpole was perhaps the first genuine prime minister. Other PM names of the Georgian era, of course, include Pitt the Elder and Pitt the Younger. Then, in the nineteenth century, there were big-name PMs such as Disraeli and Gladstone. And in the twentieth century, among others – Churchill, Attlee, Wilson and Thatcher. It's hard to know yet which, if any, of Downing Street's early twenty-first-century occupants will make it into history's eventual list of really famous PMs.

IT'S NOT CALLED A KINGDOM FOR NOTHING

There have been monarchs (and monarchs' ministers) in England for a very long time now and, inevitably, they have left their mark on the fabric of life here today. They have made their mark sometimes in a very physical form.

The currency, for instance, has long carried a portrait of the monarch. Some of the heads portrayed on pre-Roman coins might be intended as portraits. Certainly, there were Anglo-Saxon kings who had their faces on their coinage. It was a useful method of informing people with very limited access to news who their monarch was. And the monarch has been on coins ever since (apart from during the Commonwealth, obviously).

On a grander scale, across England there are spectacular buildings constructed by or occupied by the monarchs who ruled here. There are, of course, massive royal castles, such as the Tower of London and Windsor Castle. Then there are the great palaces, such as the Palace of St James and, of course, Buckingham Palace. In addition, there are lots of other types of buildings that have received royal patronage.

And the monarchs who ruled here have left their mark on so many of the major institutions created by them and under them. Monarchy has, of course, had a long connection with the military, since the days when monarchs would literally lead their armies into battle. However, there are also many royal cultural, charitable, scientific and other types of institutions too.

3

A SURPRISING NUMBER OF REBELS

A lot of people round the world think of England as a calm, law-abiding country in which people go about their lives and business obeying the rules, with little or no complaining. To some extent, that's how we English see ourselves too.

We are, for instance, well known for our enthusiasm for orderly queuing. However, when you look more closely at what England is today and has been over the centuries, you'd have to admit that there is also a big rebellious streak in our nature.

A lot of these rebels, of course, have been the traditional type of rebel – people carrying sharp metal objects and determined to change the government – however, there has been over the centuries rebelliousness in pretty much every aspect of society in England.

REBELS TO REPEL INVASION

We have already mentioned Boudicca, one of the most famous rebels in the region that would become England. Even today, you can see a Victorian interpretation of her and her daughters on a chariot charging along the Embankment towards the Houses of Parliament. She looks very fierce and formidable, and not prepared to take any affront from people claiming to rule her, and the MPs who sit in the Houses of Parliament are probably quite glad she's just a statue.

Boudicca was rebelling against a violent, oppressive invader. Another rebel in England also doing that – and this time, an actual English rebel – was Hereward the Wake. He was an Anglo-Saxon nobleman who, after the Norman invasion, established himself on the Isle of Ely in the East Anglian fenland, which in those days was pretty much an isle. From there, he fought the invaders. Nobody is sure what happened to him, although clearly the Normans won in the end. And nobody really knows why he is called 'the Wake', although it may mean 'watchful' which, as a rebel, can be a pretty useful trait.

NOBLES, REBELS, BARONS

During the Middle Ages there were, of course, a lot of aristocratic rebels in England. In a world where aristocrats could easily be richer than the monarch and could think they had a better claim to the throne than the actual monarch, it was pretty much inevitable that every so often one of them would try his hand at replacing the monarch or at least acquiring more power over the monarch.

We have already mentioned the 'barons' who caused such trouble to medieval English kings, and such aristocratic rebellions continued into Tudor times. For instance, in 1554, in Wyatt's Rebellion, three knights and a duke rebelled against Queen Mary. And in 1569, the Revolt of the Northern Earls against Queen Elizabeth took place. Not a great success for the Northern Earls: they were soon dead or in exile. Queen Elizabeth would still be on the throne until her death in 1603.

ORDINARY PEOPLE, EXTRAORDINARY VENTURES

However, it wasn't just the rich who were rebelling. Certainly not. Lots of other people were at it too.

In 1381, for instance, a lot of peasants rebelled in what has become known, unsurprisingly, as the Peasants' Revolt. Being a peasant in the Middle Ages wasn't much fun, and it was even less fun when the government tried to impose extra taxes on you. In 1381, a bunch of peasants in the east of England decided they had had enough and marched on London. Leaders of the 1381 rebellion included Wat Tyler, Jack Straw (no, not the Labour minister under Blair, but, yes, the Jack Straw in the pub name Jack Straw's Castle in Hampstead, which was named after a place where the rebel leader was said to have taken refuge) and the radical preacher John Ball, who famously preached, 'When Adam delved and Eve span, who was then the gentleman?'

The rebellion caught the government at what was, for the government, an awkward time. King Richard II was only 14 and a lot of government forces were elsewhere, either in the north or in France. The rebels took control of parts of London and forced King Richard to agree to abolish serfdom and accept several of their other demands. However, eventually Wat Tyler was killed in a scuffle and, as royal reinforcements mustered, the rebel force in London collapsed.

Rebels elsewhere in England were dealt with piecemeal by pro-government forces. The Establishment had managed to continue clinging to power – as the Establishment usually does, which is why it's the Establishment.

The Peasants' Revolt of 1381 is probably the most famous of these rebellions, but it certainly wasn't the only one. For instance, in 1450, there was Jack Cade's Rebellion.

This took place just before the Wars of the Roses. England was about to lose the Hundred Years War and there was, for that and for other reasons, a widespread perception both among aristocrats and among those less wealthy that the government of Henry VI was weak, corrupt and generally rubbish. Little is known about Jack Cade, but he led an army of unhappy men towards London, demanding the removal of traitors in the government.

Cade and his men managed to seize parts of London, but eventually Londoners responded and fought a battle with the rebels on London Bridge, forcing them to retreat. The authorities then used the lure of pardons to split the rebels and Cade was mortally wounded in a skirmish. It could be a tough life and a quick death being a rebel.

In 1497, large parts of Cornwall rebelled. Cornwall is part of England in the sense that Cornwall is not these days generally recognised as a country separate from England. On the other hand, people of Anglo-Saxon heritage had at that stage only ever been a small minority in Cornwall, and Cornish was still widely spoken. In the 1497 rebellion, increased taxation was again a grievance and to this was added the fact that the new King Henry VII had suspended some of the existing privileges of the tin industry, which was vital to the area.

A rebel force headed east from Cornwall, picking up some support en route. Led by blacksmith Michael Joseph, or Michael An Gof, lawyer Thomas Flamank and James Touchet, Baron Audley, the force advanced on London. However, by the time the rebel force began its advance into London, Henry VII had assembled a large royal army. In the Battle of Deptford Bridge the rebels were defeated and its three leaders were later executed. It was a long journey from Cornwall, which at the time didn't seem to achieve much but, after a period of initial royal reprisal, it would make the monarchy in London a little more wary of upsetting Cornwall in future and it still inspires some proud Cornish people today.

Later in 1497, Perkin Warbeck, claiming to be the younger of the princes in the tower and, therefore, claiming to have more right to the throne than Henry VII, acquired a lot of supporters in Cornwall and captured Exeter. However, in the end, Warbeck himself was captured by Henry's forces and the second Cornish rebellion of 1497 collapsed.

Henry VIII's departure from the Catholic Church and his creation of the Church of England added a whole new list of reasons that some people might want to rebel. The 1536 Pilgrimage of Grace happened in the north of England. The rebels had economic grievances but were also upset about Henry's attack on the Catholic Church in England, which is why the rebellion has a religious name; it wasn't led by a person called Grace. The rebels seized York but then disbanded when they thought their demands had been met. Not a wise move, as it turned out, because it allowed Henry VIII to seize the rebellion's leaders and execute them.

In 1549, early in the reign of Edward VI, there was yet another rebellion in Cornwall, the Prayer Book Rebellion. Again, the rebels were driven by a mix of economic and religious motivations. A major grievance was the attempted introduction of *The Book of Common Prayer* in English, which was intended to replace Latin texts. There were also, however, some explicitly social motivations. Some rebels wanted to 'Kill the gentlemen'.

The rebels laid siege to Exeter and a series of bitter battles were fought against Crown forces, ending in decisive defeat for the rebels at the Battle of Sampford Courtenay in Devon.

However, even while the Cornish Prayer Book Rebellion was happening, other rebels with solely economic grievances were taking up arms on the other side of the island. In 1549, Kett's Rebellion threw Norfolk into chaos. Kett, a prosperous local farmer, led a rebel army angered by enclosures forcing locals off common land. The rebels seized Norwich and subsequently defeated a royal army in fierce fighting in city streets. A second attack by a stronger royal army, however, crushed the rebellion and Kett was convicted of treason and hanged from the walls of Norwich Castle.

The Civil War involving King Charles I was, of course, as we have already seen, one enormous English rebellion with other rebellions in Scotland and Ireland. And the replacement of James II with William and Mary in 1688 was a major act of English rebellion but did also include a major foreign invasion.

In many senses, the last major English armed rebellion could be said to have been the Monmouth Rebellion in 1685. Its final

IN 1549 A D ROBERT KETT YEOMAN FARMER OF WYMONDHAM WAS EXECUTED BY HANGING IN THIS CASTLE AFTER THE DEFEAT OF THE NORFOLK REBELLION OF WHICH HE WAS THE LEADER IN 1949 A D · FOUR HUNDRED YEARS LATER · THIS MEMORIAL WAS PLACED HERE BY THE CITIZENS OF NORWICH IN REPARATION AND HONOUR TO A NOTABLE AND COURAGEOUS LEADER IN THE LONG STRUGGLE OF THE COMMON PEOPLE OF ENGLAND TO ESCAPE FROM A SERVILE LIFE INTO THE FREEDOM OF JUST CONDITIONS

battle, the Battle of Sedgemoor, is often said to have been the last major battle on English soil.

In many senses, the Monmouth Rebellion was a precursor of events in 1688, but with a very different outcome. The Duke of Monmouth was the eldest son of Charles II, but his mother was Lucy Walter, not the wife of the king (who was Catherine of Braganza), so he had never been the acknowledged heir to the throne, who was James, brother of Charles and a Catholic.

When Charles II died in early 1685, James became James II. Monmouth set off from the Netherlands soon after with the intention of replacing James on the throne. He landed with a few men at Lyme Regis. The port had yet to become the popular tourist destination it is now, so Monmouth did not spend any time shopping for souvenirs, writing postcards or playing on the beach. Instead, he assembled an army of local volunteers who were unenthusiastic about having James as their king and he set off on a sort of tour of the West Country, moving through Axminster, Chard, Taunton, Bridgwater, Glastonbury, Shepton Mallet and Keynsham.

He hoped to capture Bristol but feared it might be too well defended. He also failed to capture Bath and eventually retreated

westwards. The royalist army caught up with Monmouth at
Sedgemoor, where the better trained and better-equipped royal
forces slaughtered a large part of Monmouth's army. Monmouth
himself was captured in a ditch and later beheaded at Tower Hill.

ENGLISH REBELS WITHOUT A SWORD

However, you don't have to carry a sword or a gun to be a
rebel. England also has a long and interesting history of peaceful
rebels. Some of the earliest of these were religious rebels.

There's a strong streak of anti-authoritarianism in England's
religious rebels. A lot of them didn't like the wealth of the
medieval Catholic Church and they didn't appreciate that the
Catholic Church kept Latin as its main language, meaning that
in order to read most church texts and scriptures you had to be
educated, which at the time pretty much meant you had to be
wealthy or in the church.

In the late fourteenth century, Yorkshireman John Wycliffe
supervised the translation of the Bible into English. The Catholic
Church was not pleased. Even after Wycliffe died in 1384, the
Church remained very not pleased. So much so that, at the
Council of Constance in 1415, Wycliffe was condemned as a
heretic, his books were condemned to be burned, and since the
council couldn't get at a live Wycliffe, they declared that his
bones should be dug up and burned too. What was left of old
Wycliffe ended up in a nearby river.

The Catholic Church could destroy Wycliffe's bones but they
could not destroy his ideas. A group known as the Lollards
pursued some of his ideas and those of similar thinkers. Nobody
is entirely sure what the word 'Lollard' means. It may have been
a word made up by the movement's enemies and may mean
something like 'mumbler'.

Persecution of the Lollards continued through the fifteenth
century. However, in the sixteenth century, of course, the state

of religion in England was going to be transformed in a manner totally beyond the control of the Catholic Church.

Henry VIII was not naturally any kind of religious rebel. In fact, he had acquired from the Pope the title *Fidei Defensor*, Defender of the Faith, for a work he wrote in defence of the Church. (Somewhat ironically, despite the English monarchy having departed from the Catholic Church long ago, British monarchs continued using the title, abbreviated, on their coinage, and it's there – 'FID DEF' – even on the coins of Elizabeth II).

However, by the 1520s, there were plenty of religious rebels around in England, developing the Reformation ideas of Martin Luther and when Henry VIII needed a means to dump his existing queen and marry a new one, there were people on hand – like Nottinghamshire lad and then Archbishop of Canterbury, Thomas Cranmer – who were ready to help Henry achieve his goals. The Church of England was born.

The rebel Church of England, however, then quickly become the establishment that others would rebel against. Some in England remained loyal to the Catholic Church after the establishment of the Church in England and now became religious rebels themselves. It all got really complicated when Mary, during her brief reign, re-established the Catholic Church as the official church in England and the question of who was a religious rebel and who wasn't briefly changed again – and then changed yet again when Elizabeth I came in, supporting the Church of England.

In the early seventeenth century, radical religious ideas began to develop in England. Making adultery obligatory, however, wasn't one of them, despite the so-called 'Wicked Bible' being printed with the commandment 'Thou shalt commit adultery'. It seems to have been a simple typographical error and most (though not all) of the books in question were destroyed soon after printing, when the mistake was noticed.

As Charles I tried to pull the Church of England a little closer to the Catholic Church again, there were plenty who were pulling in the opposite direction. And just as the Commonwealth saw a proliferation of new religious ideas, so it also saw a proliferation of new political ideas. The Levellers wanted a fairer society with no monarchy. The Diggers decided they would build a better, fairer society by forming small rural, agrarian communities and cultivating common land. People termed (presumably by their opponents) 'the Ranters' seem to have believed in extensive moral freedom for people to do what they wished. And there were, of course, the Quakers, who quietly pursued their peaceful religion and are still with us today. There were also Muggletonians, who may have grown out of the Ranters and who were named after seventeenth-century English religious thinker Lodowicke Muggleton, not after anyone in the Harry Potter books.

During the reign of Charles II, the Church of England, to a great extent, re-established its position of authority in this land, while, in the eighteenth century, John Wesley travelled far and wide spreading his message of religious reform, which led to the creation of Methodism.

WHIG, LIBERALS AND WIGS

There would be other English religious rebels after Wesley. However, the political rebels of the Commonwealth had been, to some extent, a sign of what was to come and (mostly) peaceful political and social rebels would now become a major factor in the development of England and English society.

In the late seventeenth century, during the reign of Charles II, who was restored to the throne after the Commonwealth, political thinker Algernon Sidney wrote in support of restoring the Commonwealth instead. His *Discourses Concerning Government*, with its support for the need for popular consent for government (which seems uncontroversial now but was then radical indeed), would become hugely influential. When, however, he was implicated in a plot to remove Charles he was executed.

Around at the same time was John Locke, sometimes known as the 'father of liberalism'. Again, his political writings would become very significant in the future of left-wing politics and his work on economics and philosophy were also very influential. Unlike so many previous rebels, he managed to not die by being executed and instead died of natural causes in 1704.

A key element in opposition to all the Stuart kings had been challenges to the concept that monarchs were ordained by God and were answerable only to God. In the late seventeenth and early eighteenth centuries English politics divided into those more inclined to support the power of the monarch and those who wanted to restrict the power of the monarch and give more power to Parliament. The latter faction became known as Whigs.

The name is somewhat confusing. This all came at a time when actual enormous wigs were being worn by both men and women. However, the name Whigs is not connected to wigs – wearing wigs at the time was not some left-wing fashion. In fact, the word Whigs seems to be derived from a word for Scottish cattle dealers and was probably first used by the opponents of the liberal Whig politicians and was intended as an insult to them. Equally, of course, the word Tory seems to come from a word for Irish rebels and, again, when originally used in English politics was intended as an insult. The use of political insults has a very long history in England.

During the eighteenth century, as already noted, it eventually was a prime minister in Parliament who controlled the daily running of the country, rather than the monarch, and the Whigs became the dominant force in Westminster politics for a while. It would be wise to avoid viewing most Whigs as liberal by today's standards. This, after all, was a period when the British Empire was growing and the use of slaves was increasing.

Nevertheless, by the end of the century, some political rebels were making great advances in their thinking. There was admiration in some quarters for the egalitarian principles of the French and American Revolutions. In the 1780s, the Quakers had set up anti-slavery committees and, in 1787, the Society for Effecting the Abolition of the Slave Trade was founded. Soon, Yorkshireman William Wilberforce would be promoting the arguments for abolishing slavery.

In 1792, Mary Wollstonecraft's *A Vindication of the Rights of Woman*, hugely influential in the development of feminism, was published, stating that women are just as good as men, something that seems obvious now, but was very radical at the time. Her daughter Mary Shelley went on to write *Frankenstein*, which was, yes, a little less influential in the development of feminism, but is still definitely one of the most famous books ever.

During the nineteenth century, the political rebels kept on developing their ideas and advancing their campaigns. Slavery in the Empire was eventually abolished. By this stage, Parliament had been around a long time, but there were restrictions on who could vote and who could be an MP, which meant that Parliament didn't have much connection with normal people.

In 1819, a mass meeting was called at St Peter's Field in Manchester to demand electoral reform. The response of the local magistrates was to send in the cavalry. Eventually, hussars charged the crowd with sabres drawn and a number of people were killed and hundreds were injured. The Battle of Waterloo had happened only four years before and the event has gone down in history as the infamous Peterloo Massacre.

Undeterred, people kept on demanding electoral reform. In 1838, a committee of six MPs and six working men produced the 'People's Charter'. It demanded a series of six reforms, most of which, such as the secret ballot, seem familiar today. Interestingly, one of the demands of the charter that still has not been met is a demand for annual parliamentary elections. Perhaps we should now try it!

The supporters of the Charter became known as Chartists. A series of marches, demonstrations, riots and even an attempted national rebellion followed as the Chartists tried to get their demands met and the authorities resisted stubbornly and ferociously. In the end, Chartism collapsed, but almost all its demands would eventually be met later in the nineteenth and early twentieth centuries.

The Whigs became the Liberals and Liverpudlian William Ewart Gladstone became the most famous Liberal PM of the nineteenth century, bringing in reforming measures such as the Education Act of 1870, which set up state-run elementary schools, and the Trade Union Act of 1871, which legalised trade unions.

ENGLISH REBELS EVERYWHERE!

In the early nineteenth century, the so-called Luddites had been a labour movement that had destroyed machines that workers feared would make them lose their jobs. The Luddites were, much like so many other movements that were launched by ordinary people, ruthlessly suppressed by the authorities.

In 1834, the Tolpuddle Martyrs suffered penal transportation to Australia after forming an agricultural union in their home village, which happened to be, yes, Tolpuddle in Dorset. However, even in those times, the punishment was seen by many as outrageous and after mass marches and petitions in their support, the Martyrs were pardoned in 1836 and allowed to return to England.

After their legalisation in 1871, labour movements continued to develop in the late nineteenth century, as, of course, did socialism. Admittedly neither Karl Marx nor Friedrich Engels were English, but England did play a major part in the origins of socialism and communism.

Karl Marx lived in London for much of his life; he often worked in the British Museum Reading Room and is buried in Highgate Cemetery. Engels' father owned textile factories in

Salford and Engels spent a chunk of his life in Manchester, and some time in London and that was where eventually he died.

Socialism drew both upon theoretical works, such as those of Marx and Engels, but also on the practical experiences of those, such as the Chartists, who were working towards a more egalitarian society. In 1884, the Fabian Society, which wanted a peaceful movement towards a socialist country, was founded in London. It still exists today, and the society would also help found the Labour Party.

And so we reach the Suffragettes. The word is nothing to do with suffering, although suffer some of the Suffragettes did, during their campaign of civil disobedience aimed at winning the vote for women. Instead, the word is derived from the Latin word *suffragium*, which means votes. As we have already seen happen elsewhere in political history, Suffragette was a word originally intended as an insult that was later proudly adopted by the people it was intended to diminish.

There had been calls for some time for women to get the vote and in 1903 Mancunian Emmeline Pankhurst formed the Women's Social and Political Union to campaign more actively for that. This began a campaign of marches, meetings, demonstrations and political events. Women chained themselves to railings, shouted at politicians and attempted to storm Parliament itself. One campaigner, Emily Davison, was killed intervening in the Derby.

The originally peaceful campaign began to involve more violent events. Windows were smashed, there was arson and even small explosions. The state reacted, as it often had done before to rebels, ruthlessly. Many Suffragettes were imprisoned and when some of them went on hunger strike, force feeding was introduced. Eventually, though, the state had had enough. In 1918, the Representation of the People Act was passed, introducing categories of women who were eligible to vote and widening the categories of men eligible to vote.

In 1914 the First World War arrived. A lot of people today tend to think of an England and a Britain united in the war effort. This, however, ignores the pacifist rebels who refused, for moral reasons, to fight. Hundreds of war resisters were imprisoned here and others would later be imprisoned for resisting fighting in the Second World War.

The Russian Revolution in 1917 encouraged the spread of Communist ideals in England. There were even some links to the Suffragette campaign. Sylvia Pankhurst, the daughter of Emmeline Pankhurst, became, in 1920, leader of the Communist Party (British Section of the Third International). However, multiple internal disputes and the strength and success of the Labour Party meant that Communism was only ever a minority pursuit in England. It was perhaps at its strongest during the period of the Spanish Civil War when left-wing volunteers from England and elsewhere went, against the wishes of the government here, to Spain to fight Fascism.

It's worth mentioning a few of the English volunteers. Tom Wintringham, from Lincolnshire, rose to be commander of the British Battalion of the International Brigades and, afterwards, during the Second World War, helped develop tactics for the Local Defence Volunteers and Home Guard. Jack Jones suffered major wounds in the Battle of the Ebro and went on to become General Secretary of the Transport and Workers' Union and one of the most powerful people in 1970s Britain. Olympic gold medallist in rowing Lewis Clive became a company commander and was killed in battle in 1938. George Orwell served as a volunteer in the Marxist POUM (Workers' Party of Marxist Unification) and was wounded in the throat, later writing *Homage to Catalonia* as a record of his time in Spain. The post-Second World War era is, of course, well known for its rebels and rebellions.

In the middle of the Cold War, when nuclear obliteration of the world seemed a genuine possibility, the rebels of CND, the Campaign for Nuclear Disarmament, marched and demonstrated in favour of a world free of nuclear weapons. A lot of their early efforts were against AWRE, the Atomic Weapons Research Establishment at Aldermaston in Berkshire. Out of the movement came the classic peace symbol, which looks like a cross with dropped arms in a circle. It was designed by Gerald Holtom, who grew up in Holt in Norfolk and was inspired by the semaphore signals for 'N' and 'D' (the initial letters of Nuclear Disarmament).

The post-war period was to see huge changes in the lives of women, as female rebels stood up and demanded their rights. The introduction of the contraceptive pill in the 1960s and 1970s gave women more reproductive and sexual freedom. In 1968, women machinists at the Ford Factory in Dagenham went on strike demanding equal pay with their male colleagues. In 1970, the first Women's Liberation Movement national conference was held in Oxford with over 600 women attending. The same year, a group of female rebels disrupted the Miss World competition in London. In 1975, the Sex Discrimination Act was passed. The battle for sexual equality is not yet won, but huge advances have been made.

And women weren't the only oppressed group rebelling at the time. Racist discrimination was not even illegal here until 1965. Even after it was banned, there was still extensive discrimination against immigrant groups. The Grunwick Strike, in London in 1976, was the first major strike in which a largely immigrant workforce (mainly women of South Asian heritage who had come to England from East Africa) took on management with the support of the main labour movement. Organisations such as the Black Peoples' Alliance were formed to defend communities and promote their interests. In 1981, the Black People's Day of Action took place in London. Campaigning against racism continues.

Homosexual acts were illegal in the UK until 1967 and, even after that, discrimination was widespread. In 1970 the Gay Liberation Front was founded and in 1972 the first Pride march took place. From the 1970s onwards, and continuing today, LGBT+ rebels have campaigned for equality and respect and their campaigns continue.

In recent years, environmental concerns have inspired a particularly significant number of rebels. Stroud, in Gloucestershire, may not seem a hugely radical location, but in 2018 it produced Extinction Rebellion, which has gone on to be a major force in the world of environmental campaigning and of campaigning generally.

Every country and culture around the world, of course, has its rebels, but there is perhaps something particularly in English culture and society that is instinctively rebellious, something that takes a natural delight in resisting conformity and regimentation. We have certainly produced a LOT of rebels over the centuries.

4

MAKING FRIENDS WITH THE NEIGHBOURS – OR NOT

England isn't the whole world. It isn't even the whole island. Some people would like to think England is the whole world (or at least the whole island) and they are called Little Englanders. This, however, is not *The Book of Little England*, it is *The Little Book of England*, so now we're going to have a very brief look at some of the fun England has had with its neighbours on this planet and, inevitably, some of the less fun bits as well.

THE WELSH NEXT DOOR

The Welsh are very close neighbours to England, but the situation between the two sometimes hasn't been an easy one. The word 'Welsh' itself is derived from a probably rather derogatory Anglo-Saxon word for non-Anglo-Saxons. However, in this instance, a word that was originally perhaps meant to be uncomplimentary was, eventually, proudly adopted by the Welsh themselves as something much more positive. The same, however, can't be said of the term 'welshing' or 'welching' on a deal. The origins of the phrase are somewhat disputed, but it's a phrase to be avoided.

England, of course, spent quite a lot of time invading Wales in the Middle Ages, and many of the great castles that we think of as Welsh castles, such as Harlech and Conwy, are actually English castles built to impose English rule on Wales – although it does get even more confusing when we get to Caernarfon, which was built by Edward I but is thought by some to have been designed to resemble the walls of Constantinople, then the capital of the Byzantine Empire and now Istanbul in Turkey.

Caernarfon is also, of course, linked with the whole Prince of Wales question. Having slaughtered existing Welsh princes of Wales, Edward I declared his son, born at Caernarfon, as Prince of Wales. Since that time, the heir to the throne of England (and subsequently the heir to the throne of the United Kingdom) has traditionally been the Prince of Wales, even though most of them haven't been very Welsh at all. Edward I's son, the first Prince of Wales, for instance, spent very little time in Wales. The investiture of Prince Charles (now Charles III) as Prince of Wales took place at Caernarfon in 1969.

The English have sometimes not shown much respect for Welsh culture. For instance, in the sixteenth century English was promoted in Wales as the language of government and officialdom, while the Welsh Language was supressed. However, more recently, Welsh literary stars such as Dylan Thomas and Welsh music stars like Shirley Bassey and, of course, Tom Jones have become huge in England. So that's a positive change at least and at last.

ISLAND OF THE BEE GEES

The Man in the name Isle of Man is not English 'man'. So, it's not Isle of Man, like Brotherhood of Man (who were winners of the Eurovision in 1976 and who were not all men). Instead, the word has Celtic roots and is perhaps a word for mount or mountain.

A lot of people have invaded the Isle of Man. In 1290, Edward I, taking a brief rest from invading other places, ordered an English invasion of the Isle of Man. There was then a bit of the Scots taking it, followed by the English taking it, followed by the Scots taking it, followed by the English taking it, etc. You get the picture.

Barry Gibb, Maurice Gibb and Robin Gibb of the Bee Gees were all born on the Isle of Man. A lot of people around the world think they were born in the USA.

THE EMERALD ISLE

Clearly, England has a long and (very) complicated history with Ireland, much of it involving England invading Ireland or ruling Ireland badly, and most of it beyond the remit of this little book. There are a lot of scars in there, including, of course, those caused by the horrific Irish Potato Famine.

In the twelfth century, the Anglo-Norman invasion of Ireland started, creating the Lordship of Ireland. In 1542, Henry VIII was declared King of Ireland, and the monarchs of England (and then Britain) were also monarchs of Ireland until 1801 when the United Kingdom of Great Britain and Ireland was declared.

In fact, Ireland had never been that united with Great Britain, and by 1922, after assorted fighting, it was even less united. Most of Ireland left British control in that year and the United Kingdom of Great Britain and Northern Ireland was declared instead in 1927.

The city frequently known these days as just Derry is also called sometimes Londonderry because in 1613 London guild companies took a major role in establishing new settlements in the area, and they were allowed to add London to the existing name, Derry.

If you asked a lot of people to give the name of an English general of the twentieth century, most of them would probably say Montgomery, old Monty. Montgomery was indeed born in Kennington, London, but his father was a Church of Ireland minister and member of a family of gentry from the northern end of Ireland. Monty's grandfather Sir Robert Montgomery was born at the family estate at Moville, Inishowen, in County Donegal.

Recent Irish people loved by the English (and others) include Val Doonican, Terry Wogan, Graham Norton and the Corrs.

NORTH OF THE BORDER

The English have spent quite a lot of time invading Scotland, but then the Scottish have also spent quite a lot of time invading England. As mentioned in Chapter 1, Gildas was already, in the sixth century, complaining about people from what is now Scotland invading what is now England. And the epic poem 'Y Gododdin', written sometime between the seventh and eleventh centuries, is about raiders sometime around the year 600, feasting in Edinburgh and then heading south to attack a place that is often identified as Catterick in Yorkshire.

The English were invading Scotland a lot earlier than many people will know. When people think of English invasions of Scotland, a lot of them, obviously, think of *Braveheart*, with Mel Gibson (born in the USA, grew up in Australia), with his face painted half blue and lots of thirteenth-century knights. However, the English were probably attacking Edinburgh as early as 638 and by 685 they had pushed even further north but were then defeated by the Picts at the Battle of Nechtansmere.

Lots more wars between Scots and English were to follow, including, of course, those involving William Wallace and Robert the Bruce. In 'Flower of Scotland', sung so enthusiastically by Scottish rugby fans at Scotland versus England rugby matches, the lyrics refer to King Edward being sent home to England after his defeat by Robert the Bruce. Berwick upon Tweed was sometimes Scottish, sometimes English (it's English now).

Then, as already mentioned, Scottish King James VI became king of both Scotland and England and became, somewhat confusingly, James VI and I. The grandson of James VI and I was another King James, James VII and II. Now James in Latin is *Jacobus*. So, when James II got chucked off the throne in 1688, those thinking he and his heirs should still be on it were called, yes of course, Jacobites.

All this led to probably the most famous invasion of England by the Scots, Bonny Prince Charlie's excursion to Derbyshire with a Jacobite army in 1745. Lovely though much of Derbyshire is, that wasn't really his planned destination. However, he wasn't entirely sure of the reception he would receive further south, and in the end he returned to Scotland to a huge defeat at Culloden and exile again. There was then brutal repression in Scotland after the defeat of the rebellion.

However, soon it would all get a bit more friendly between the English and Scots. Queen Victoria loved Scotland. She also loved her hubby, Prince Albert. They first went to Scotland in 1842, just a couple of years after getting married and less than a century after Culloden, and they fell in love with Deeside. Albert thought it looked like a bit of Germany he was fond of, and Victoria loved the isolation and quietness.

So, yes, she had Balmoral Castle built, still a treasured holiday home of the British royals. And she loved the idea of Scottishness. She loved tartan and whisky and Highland games and Highland dancing. She started the Ghillies Ball at Balmoral, which continues today. After Prince Albert's death, she also seems to have loved her own Scottish servant or ghillie, John Brown.

Scottish culture had not previously been generally very popular in England. Samuel Johnson, in his seventeenth century dictionary, notoriously described oats as something that in England was usually given to horses, but in Scotland was eaten by the people, and after Culloden measures were taken to prohibit the wearing of tartan.

However, all that (or much of it) soon changed. In the nineteenth century Queen Victoria was a fashion leader. If she liked it, a lot of other people were going to like it too. Suddenly, Scottishness became a bit fashionable in England and other rich English people went to the Highlands to experience it all.

The Scots have, of course, never lost their proud sense of identity. And that has continued to be expressed, among other means, through sport. Traditionally, matches between England and Scotland, particularly football and rugby matches, have seen very fierce competition. Each year, the England and Scotland rugby teams compete for the Calcutta Cup. This is decorated with an elephant and cobras – not found widely in either England or Scotland – because the tradition of England versus Scotland rugby matches started in India in the nineteenth century.

Teams representing England and Scotland first started playing football against each other in 1870, and the matches have seen some astonishing incidents. Among the most famous – or infamous – is the match in 1977 when Scotland beat England at Wembley and Scottish fans invaded the pitch, grabbed bits of the turf and broke the goalposts.

James Bond instantly says Englishness to a lot of people around the world. Perhaps the most famous Bond (and arguably the best) was Sean Connery, who was famously Scottish.

THE HOME OF BERGERAC

Not all islands in the Channel are Channel Islands (though maybe those are Channel islands with a small 'i'). The Isle of

Wight is part of England; Jersey, Guernsey, Sark and Alderney are not.

The Channel Islands used to be part of the Duchy of Normandy and, in some sense, are the last bit of the French empire that English monarchs used to control. The islands do, therefore, as people who have visited will mostly know, still have a bit of a French flavour. Some older war monuments carry text in French and there are still a lot of surnames with French origins, such as the name of Detective Bergerac, for instance. (OK, yes, Bergerac was a fictional detective, but there are also lots of genuine French surnames on the islands.)

The Channel Islands also have, over the centuries, acquired quite an English flavour as well. In 1940, the British Government decided that after the Germans had occupied northern France, defending the Channel Islands would be impossible, and so the Germans occupied the Channel Islands as well. Photos of German troops marching past Lloyds Bank or standing next to British policemen still look very strange.

LA BELLE FRANCE

And since we have done the Channel Islands, we might as well now cross that short stretch of water and land in England's old adversary and new friend (sort of). Yes, it's '*Bonjour* France'.

It's hard to be exactly sure when the rivalry between England and France began. In the pre-Roman period there were extensive cross-Channel ties. During the Roman period, both lands were part of the same empire. And in the post-Roman period, the Franks had close links with the Anglo-Saxon Kingdom of Kent.

The Norman conquest of 1066 did inevitably cause a lot of resentment in England, but then the Normans weren't entirely French. Soon after the invasion, French would become one of the languages frequently used by the rich and posh in Norman England. And, of course, medieval English monarchs had a French empire. At one stage, England almost had a French king, and at another stage, an Englishman almost sat on the French throne.

Yes, England's defeat at the end of the Hundred Years War and the loss of its French empire must have caused resentment too, but by the reign of Elizabeth I, it was Spain, not France, that was seen as England's main continental enemy.

Perhaps it was in the eighteenth century when a lot of the English really began to dislike France. Many people in England were suspicious of the close links between the Scottish Jacobites and France, and in the early part of the century Louis XIV's France was a huge, self-confident, aggressive power just a short distance across the water from England. West Country lad John Churchill (ancestor of Winston) achieved some major victories over the armies of Louis, but the French threat did not disappear.

By the end of the eighteenth century, another Frenchman was making the English very nervous. OK, Napoleon Bonaparte was in fact Corsican, which a lot of Corsicans would regard as something very different to French, but to most English people, then (and now), he was French.

Napoleon spent a lot of time invading places, and there was a genuine fear that one of those places would be England. Defences, including lots of Martello towers, were built to defend England against any invasion by Napoleon's forces.

In the end, there was to be no invasion of England by Napoleon. However, the fear here of a French invasion did not end with Napoleon's defeat at Waterloo. In 1860, another lot of defences, the so-called Palmerston forts, were built to protect against a French invasion.

By that stage, though, some English attitudes towards the French had already begun to change. The French had been Britain's allies against the Russians in the Crimean War and France's defeat in 1870 in the Franco-Prussian War, which was followed by the proclamation of the German Empire in 1871 (under Wilhelm I who had been King of Prussia and was now

Emperor of Germany), clearly demonstrated that there was a major new power in Europe.

In 1904, Britain and France signed the Entente Cordiale that created an alliance between the two countries, partly intended to oppose German power. The timing was particularly appropriate because on the British throne at the time was Edward VII. He loved France, and indeed French women (and other women, too). He had visited France a lot. His favourite resort was Biarritz, where he took regular holidays. He was one of the major early English (well his father was German) tourists in France, but there were, of course, many more to come.

The First World War cemented the alliance between Britain and France; the Second World War created a few problems. There were mutual recriminations over events during the defeat of France in 1940 and subsequent British attacks on the forces of Vichy, the French government that collaborated with the Nazis, which was the first combat between British and French warriors in a very long time.

British support for the Resistance and for General de Gaulle, however, did a lot to repair any rift. De Gaulle himself was never a huge fan of '*les Anglo-Saxons*' (by which he meant both Brits and Americans), but after his death, the UK and France became partners in the European Union. And then there was Brexit.

Many English people, of course, love France and the French. Some are still suspicious of them, but perhaps they will be less suspicious in future. It is, after all, a long time since Louis XIV and Napoleon.

THOSE DEUTSCHLANDERS

Another of our neighbours across the sea is, of course, Germany. The question of English attitudes to Germany and the Germans is perhaps a little less complex than the whole French situation.

Germany didn't exist as a united country until that proclamation in 1871 and, prior to the late nineteenth century, nobody in England seemed particularly suspicious of Germany or the Germans. The Georgian dynasty came from Germany and Queen Victoria married a German.

The expansion of the German Empire in the late nineteenth century and, of course, the events of 1914–18 changed all that almost completely. The arrival of Hitler and the events of 1939–45 made everything a whole lot worse.

However, in the post-war era, Germany was our partner in the EU – until Brexit. And it is still our partner in NATO.

Yet suspicions can still be found in some English heads. Partly, of course, that is due to football. Yes, England beat Germany at Wembley in the 1966 World Cup Final, and yes, England beat Germany in the recent Euros. However, England has also suffered several major and very painful football defeats at the hands, or indeed the feet, of Germany.

OTHER EUROPEAN NEIGHBOURS

Well, there's Iceland, who shocked every English football fan by defeating England in the Euros in 2016 and putting them out of the competition. There are the Faroe Islands, mainly known in England, again, for occasional football performances.

There are Norway, Sweden and Denmark, collectively known in England for the Vikings (already mentioned). Sweden is known separately as the home of Abba, Volvo and Ikea.

In the 1st Battle of Copenhagen in 1801, Nelson famously turned his blind eye to the flag signal giving him the order to retreat. The horse of the Duke of Wellington (who was himself – the duke that is – Anglo-Irish) was named Copenhagen, after the 2nd Battle of Copenhagen in 1807, in which the British bombarded the Danish capital.

Then there is the country that many English call Holland, even though it's actually the Netherlands and Holland is only a small part of it. We also call the people Dutch, even though the inhabitants of the Netherlands don't call themselves that. In the seventeenth century, the Dutch were a formidable naval enemy of England. Now, they are mainly known in England for tulips and cycle lanes. A lot of Dutch people speak English; very few English people speak Dutch.

Finally, we have Belgium. Just as the most famous Channel Islander in England is a fictional detective, so the most famous Belgian in England is probably fictional detective Hercule Poirot – although Kevin De Bruyne of Manchester City, a non-fictional football player, is also very famous here now.

YANKLAND

OK, they are a bit of a distant neighbour, but there is, for instance, still only sea between Cornwall and Florida, and just as England has a long and complex history with France, so it does with the USA.

The USA today is a country that combines a vast range of ethnic, cultural and religious communities. However, the origins of the USA as a political entity are fairly English.

Obviously, before the English arrived, the original inhabitants of the land had been there a very long time. Then, in 1497, John Cabot, on his second attempt at exploring America, arrived off the coast of Newfoundland. Cabot was Italian, but he did have the support of Henry VII and some Bristol merchants, and there were probably assorted Englishmen in his expedition, as well as a Genoese barber.

Cabot's expedition probably didn't achieve that much. However, John's son, Sebastian, soon crossed the Atlantic as well. But then Henry VII died, and Henry VIII was more interested in women, feasting and jousting than sending men west.

English attempts to explore North America continued through the sixteenth century and in 1584 even got as far as Walter Raleigh establishing a settlement on Roanoke Island. By 1590, though, it was gone again.

In 1607, with James I (and VI) on the throne over here, a colony of Jamestown was established in Virginia. Eventually, the colonists worked out they could grow tobacco.

And the Puritans soon got involved in settling America. Neither James I nor Charles I were particularly keen on Puritan religious views and the Puritans realised they could find more religious freedom thousands of miles across the sea from Westminster. In 1620, the *Mayflower* turned up and set up Plymouth Colony in Cape Cod. Other Puritans were arriving elsewhere.

And then came Thanksgiving, still a huge festival in the USA, with its concept of Puritans, pilgrims and local tribes sharing food and people giving thanks to God for harvest. Of course, the European settlement of America was going to be a huge catastrophe for the peoples who had been there before the Europeans arrived. It was also going to be a huge disaster for all the Africans transported across the Atlantic to be slaves on European plantations there.

English and then British settlement in what is now the USA increased and eventually beat competition from other Europeans, particularly the French and Dutch. And then, of course, came the American Revolution in 1776, when the Brits (and other Europeans) in America decided they had had enough of being ruled by a distant George over here.

Many of the key figures in that Revolution had English heritage. John Washington, great-grandfather of George Washington, 1st President of the USA, had relocated from England in 1656. Henry Adams, the great-great-grandfather of John Adams, 2nd President of the USA, crossed the Atlantic from England in about 1638.

Since the Revolution, apart obviously from during the War of 1812 when British troops burnt the White House, English and

Americans have mostly been friends. Though, admittedly, these days, with the USA being one of the world's superpowers and the UK not quite so much, England probably tends to spend more time thinking about the USA than that country does about England.

A lot of Americans love English accents, English heritage and London. A lot of us love American food, TV, movies, jeans and music. And a lot of our politicians love American wealth and power.

THE OTHER COUNTRIES IN THE WORLD

There are, of course, lots of other countries in the world, many of them important and fascinating, but you wouldn't describe them as England's neighbours. England and the English have, of course, had links and dealings with every other country on earth. The English and British have invaded most of them (see *All the Countries We've Ever Invaded and the Few We Never Got Round To* by Stuart Laycock). However, this is the *Little Book of England*, not the *Big Book of Britain* or the *Big Book of the World*, so that story is beyond our remit here.

5

THE WORLD COMES TO ENGLAND

Britain has been invaded and occupied by Romans, Angles and Saxons, Vikings and the Normans. These invasions influenced the language and culture of the country. For almost 1,000 years, Britain has avoided invasion and instead its culture has been enriched by visitors. Merchants have come to trade, and some stayed; workers have come to help build the country; some have come as refugees to avoid dangers in the country where they were born and some just think it's a good place to live, despite the weather.

There are communities in England with heritage from every region and country of the world. To tell the story of every community in England would take a huge book, or indeed a series of huge books, and since this just the *Little Book of England*, we are going to look at three communities – Jewish, African and South East Asian.

JEWISH AND ENGLISH

England is very proud of its role in offering sanctuary to Jewish children trying to escape Nazi Germany, and 10,000 Kindertransport children arrived just before the Second World War began (see photograph of memorial in Harwich P.74). They joined about 90,000 adult Jews from Germany, Austria, Italy and Eastern Europe who fled from Nazi persecution. Today, there are over 270,000 Jewish people in England and Wales, with more than half living in London. They play an important role in English culture, but, looking back, the story of England and the Jewish community is a lot more complex.

There were probably Jewish people here during the Roman period, and more definitely arrived in England after the Norman Conquest. The Domesday Book and all that castle building required finance. William the Conqueror brought Jewish bankers from Rouen to help him fund his ambitions. In medieval Christian Europe, charging interest on loans was regarded as a sin for Christians, but Jews were allowed to charge interest on money they lent. Medieval monarchs, who had a penchant for war and displays of power, found these bankers very useful.

Licoricia of Winchester showed that Jewish women could also be successful bankers. She was one of the richest women in the thirteenth century, working alongside her second husband, David of Oxford, and then taking over his business when he died. Sadly, she came to a horrible end, being murdered and some of her money stolen. Although three men were put on trial for her murder, they were acquitted. She now has a statue in Winchester to commemorate her.

And just as Licoricia experienced both good times and an appalling death here, there is a deeply tragic side to the story of the Jewish community in medieval England.

Some people in England in the Middle Ages blamed the Jewish community for killing Jesus, and the 'Blood Libel', which was to form a powerful part of Nazi propaganda, had its origin in this country. In 1144, William of Norwich was accused of killing a young Christian boy and using his blood to prepare unleavened bread for Passover. This claim was repeated in England and across Europe when children died in unexplained situations. In 1190, it led to Jews taking refuge in Clifford's tower at York Castle, while an angry crowd bayed for their blood. Many of the Jews in the tower committed suicide and those who surrendered were murdered.

A similar incident in Bury St Edmunds saw the Jews expelled from the town and fifty-seven were killed. Many medieval barons had a vested interest in encouraging mob violence as it often destroyed the records of how much money they owed Jewish financiers.

In 1218 the Archbishop of Canterbury forced Jews to wear a badge to identify themselves. Stephen Langton chose to identify Jews with a white oblong badge, rather than the star of David as used by the Nazis, but the purpose was similar. In 1290, Edward I decided to use Italian merchants to fund his military adventures and Jews were banished from England.

Oliver Cromwell is often credited with reintroducing a Jewish community to England in 1656. By 1701, there was a Jewish synagogue at Bevis Marks, so Jews could worship openly, and at least 300 Spanish and Portuguese Jews had arrived to escape the Spanish Inquisition. Their story is mentioned in the chapter on English Food.

In the eighteenth century the Jewish community began to grow. Jewish merchants helped fund the Duke of Marlborough's wars against the Spanish, and there were other major achievements beyond the world of trade and finance. David Mendoza was England's heavyweight boxing champion between 1792 and 1795, despite weighing a mere 160lb. He is credited with making boxing more technical, focusing on side steps and blocks to outmanoeuvre opponents.

Wealthy philanthropist Moses Haim Montefiore was knighted by Queen Victoria in 1837. Benjamin Disraeli, who created the modern Conservative Party, became Britain's first Jewish prime minister in 1874. Jewish women also started businesses, including Harriet Samuel, who founded the H. Samuel jewellery chain.

In the late nineteenth century, many Ashkenazi Jews fleeing pogroms in Germany, Poland and Russia made their home here. One of the most famous of these arrivals was the novelist and author of *Heart of Darkness*, Joseph Conrad. He was born Józef Teodor Konrad Korzeniowski in modern-day Ukraine. Conrad became a British citizen in 1886 after a career in the Merchant Navy and used his maritime experiences as the basis of some of his books.

Jewish men fought bravely in the British Army in the First World War. About 50,000 Jewish men served in the armed forces and about 10,000 died. Issy Smith was born as Ishroulch Schmeilowitz in Egypt. In 1915, he won a Victoria Cross at the Second Battle of Ypres for carrying a wounded comrade to safety under heavy German fire.

The family of sprinter Harold Abrahams, whose rivalry with Eric Liddell was immortalised in the film *Chariots of Fire*, also came to England during this time. Abrahams' father fled from Poland and both his sons represented Britain in the Olympics. Sidney ran for Britain in 1912 and Harold won Olympic gold in the 100m in Paris, 1924.

In the 1930s Germany's loss was Britain's gain, as successful and talented Jews fled the Nazi regime. Sigmund Freud and his daughter Anna are among the most famous to find shelter in England, but there were many others.

For instance, Peter Moro, who designed the Royal Festival Hall, was born in Heidelberg but moved to England in 1936. Ernst Chain left Germany to help Howard Florey and Alexander Fleming develop penicillin. He shared the Nobel Prize in 1945 for his efforts.

George Weidenfeld was born in Vienna but escaped to England in 1938. When he arrived, he spoke little English but by 1942 he was broadcasting for the BBC and writing a newspaper column. After the war, he set up a publishing firm, Weidenfeld and Nicolson, and he became Baron Weidenfeld of Chelsea in 1976.

The Jewish community in England has made a huge contribution to English life, society and culture and continues to do so today. Daniel Levy, for example, is the chairman of Tottenham Hotspur and has moved the club to its magnificent new stadium. Lord Sugar, a previous chairman of Spurs, now appears regularly on his TV series, *The Apprentice*. In politics, there is former Minister for Children Margaret Hodge and in the Upper House, Lord Alf Dubs. The Miliband brothers, David and Ed, are both sons of a Belgian Jewish refugee.

Miriam Margolyes is Professor Pomona Sprout of *Harry Potter* fame and David Baddiel co-wrote the football anthem 'Three Lions'. His mother was a Jewish refugee. Comedian Ben Elton's grandfather was from the Czech Jewish community.

AFRICAN AND ENGLISH

The first Africans to arrive in England did so long ago. Roman soldiers from North Africa were stationed at Aballava on Hadrian's Wall to keep out the Picts. A little earlier, in AD 211, Roman Emperor Septimius, who had been born in Leptis Magna in Libya, died in York. Also in York, archaeologists have found the grave of a wealthy Roman lady of African descent, known as the 'ivory bangle lady'.

There were some Africans in medieval England too. Monk Richard of Devizes describes London as being a place for 'men from all nations', and Garamantes (people from North Africa) are among the groups mentioned.

As Portuguese and Spanish sailors explored the coast of Africa, searching for gold, more black people began to appear in Tudor England. Henry VIII had a black trumpeter called John Blanke, who may have arrived with Catherine of Aragon. John played at both Henry VII's funeral and Henry VIII's coronation and was sufficiently confident that he demanded Henry pay him the same as the other trumpeters. When Henry's flag ship *Mary Rose* sank in 1545, an African called Jacques Francis, who had learnt to dive collecting shells in African waters, was hired to try to rescue Henry's expensive cannons.

In the 1550s, five men were brought from Ghana to London. They came not as slaves but to learn English in the hope that this would help the English in establishing trade links. Francis Drake had an African personal assistant when he left England to circumnavigate the globe in 1577.

And this is where we reach the shameful tragedy that was England's involvement in the slave trade. Tudor slave trading was a comparatively small-scale affair. However, by the end of the seventeenth century, England would be making a lot of money from both transporting slaves across the Atlantic and forcing them to work on plantations.

In 1627, the English settled in Barbados and began growing sugar cane. It was a profitable business because sugar was a luxury in England, but producing it was hard work and required a lot of people. Initially, plantation owners bought slaves from foreign traders.

In 1660, Charles II and his son, James, set up the Royal African Company and gave it a monopoly on trading slaves. The 1661 Barbados Slave Code divided the island into free 'Whites' and enslaved 'Blacks', with different laws for each.

Slaves were the property of their owner and these rules spread quickly to other colonies in America and the West Indies. Captains of slave ships were allowed to bring a few slaves back to England, where they sold them to wealthy families as servants.

However, the eighteenth century also saw some black people escaping slavery and making a name for themselves. Bill Richmond, for example, began life as a slave on Staten Island, New York. During the American War of Independence, he fought for the Brits. His commanding officer, the Earl of Northumberland, brought him to England and funded his apprenticeship as a cabinetmaker. Bill then became a bodyguard to Lord Camelford, who introduced him to boxing. When Camelford died, Bill became a professional boxer, despite being in his forties. He set up a boxing school and trained Lord Byron, among others. He turned up alongside other boxers as an usher at the coronation of George IV. He was still boxing in his sixties.

Julius Soubisse was freed from slavery by his owner, Catherine Douglas, Duchess of Queensberry. He learnt to fence and became an expert horseman. He liked to call himself 'The Black Prince' and was well known in London's high society.

The slave trade became illegal in 1807, but it was not until 1833 that the British abolished slavery itself. Although William Wilberforce is often credited with this achievement, many black people were also fighting hard for their freedom.

Olaudah Equiano published his life story in 1789. It became a bestseller, and his book tours showed his readers the cruelty of life on the plantations. Ottobah Cugoano was born in Ghana, shipped to Grenada as a slave and freed in London. In 1787, he joined with Equiano to form the Sons of Africa. Alongside other former slaves, they campaigned to abolish slavery. Letters were written, speaking tours undertaken and pamphlets produced to show the injustice of slavery.

Mary Prince was perhaps the first ex-slave to make public a female perspective on life as a slave. Ignatius Sancho was born on a slave ship in the Atlantic and was brought to England as a baby. He taught himself to read and write and to compose music. In 1773, he opened a grocer's shop in Westminster, where he met well-known artists, writers and politicians. He campaigned for an end to slavery and became the first black man to vote in 1774.

The end of slavery did not mean an end to prejudice against black people but, in the period after it, the black community did become more prominent in English life. Mary Seacole, for instance, who was born in Jamaica, set up her British Hotel in the Crimea to nurse British soldiers at the same time as Florence Nightingale

The trend continued in the twentieth century. Huge numbers of men of African and Caribbean heritage fought for Britain in both world wars. Walter Tull had played professional football for Tottenham and Northampton before enlisting in 1914. He was promoted to sergeant and fought at the Somme before returning to Britain for officer training. He fought at Ypres and died shortly before the end of the war in 1918. He was the first black officer to lead white men in combat (see photograph of statue of Walter Tull in Northampton, opposite).

Dr John Aleindor was one of the first qualified black doctors in London and applied to join the Royal Medical Corps in 1914. He was turned down and worked for the Red Cross instead, helping wounded soldiers as they returned to London from the trenches.

Ulric Cross from Trinidad joined the RAF in 1941, flying eighty bombing missions over Europe and being awarded the Distinguished Flying Cross.

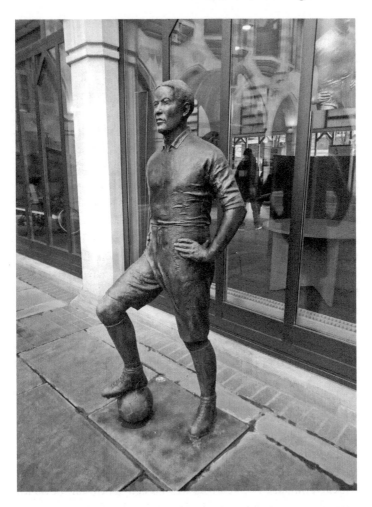

Women volunteered too. Lilian Bader joined the Women's Auxiliary Airforce after being asked to leave her job in an army canteen because she was black. The RAF were slightly less racist and she spent the war repairing aircraft instruments.

When the war ended Britain had a lot of rebuilding to do and appealed to Commonwealth countries for help. In June 1948, the *Empire Windrush* arrived from Jamaica, carrying people who were anxious to settle in Britain and help. This began a period of mass migration where about 500,000 black people arrived to work in jobs like British Transport and the NHS. They experienced a lot of discrimination, which was stirred up by politicians such as Enoch Powell and others. Even today, some of the Windrush Generation have had to fight for their right to stay in Britain.

The 2021 Census listed 2.4 million Brits as black. They have made an enormous contribution to all aspects of life, culture and commerce in England. Bruce Oldfield is, for instance, a major fashion entrepreneur. Sir Lenny Henry and Baroness Floella Benjamin are outstanding on TV. Stormzy was the first grime artist to have a number one album. Benjamin Zephaniah is often in the media reading his poetry. Andrea Levy is a prize-winning novelist. Claudia Jones began the Notting Hill Carnival. Black English footballers like Marcus Rashford play a huge part in the game here. And, of course, there is Lewis Hamilton, who dominated F1 for years.

SOUTH ASIAN AND ENGLISH

What has Rishi Sunak got in common with Priti Patel and Suella Braverman? Obviously, all three were members of Boris Johnson's recent Conservative Government and have played leading roles in recent political controversies, but also all three have Indian heritage and have held very senior positions in the UK Government. Their careers are one sign of how far the South Asian community has come in England and in Britain.

After the Spanish Armada in 1588, English sailors began to look for trade routes to India and the Far East. The East India Company (EIC) was granted a royal charter by Queen Elizabeth in 1600 with the aim of developing the spice trade. By 1620, it had established a toehold in India, trading cotton, silk, indigo and saltpetre. It was on the ships of the EIC that the first people from India travelled to England.

Indian names begin appearing in English records in the seventeenth century. Samuel Munsur is recorded as marrying Jane Johnson in Deptford in 1613. The Munsur name suggests he was Asian. Five years later, 'James', an Indian servant to the brewer Mr James Duppa, appears in Aldgate burial records. A painting of Lady Charlotte Fitzroy from 1672 shows her being offered grapes by an Indian boy.

By the eighteenth century, the EIC was wealthy and working for the company was an attractive proposition for an ambitious young Englishman. As more Brits headed to India to make their fortunes, they employed more Asian servants to make their lives comfortable.

Local nursemaids, known as *ayah*s, were employed by English families in India, and many were specifically hired for the voyage back to England. When the journey was over, some continued their employment, but many were left homeless, waiting for work on outbound ships. Rules were introduced to try to ensure they were given a return ticket, but the rules were not properly enforced. The EIC was unwilling to offer the women free passage home abut it feared that its reputation would be damaged if there were too many Asian women homeless by the docks. Some hostels were established, but the women themselves were resourceful and often managed to find their own solutions.

Finding sailors for EIC ships on their journeys back to England was often problematic. Conditions were poor and mortality rates high. It was not uncommon for 20 per cent of the crew to die and some sailors decided to remain in India rather than return home. The solution, the EIC found, was to use local sailors known as *lascars*. When the ships reached England, these sailors were again often discharged and left to fend for themselves.

In the nineteenth century, more South Asians began to settle in England. Among those mentioned in the records are singers and musicians, gardeners, sellers of spices, even a photographer, Albert Mahomet.

Soon, South Asians were also starting to do professional jobs. Sake Dean Mahomed opened a bath house in Brighton in 1814, offering therapeutic massages and shampoo baths. One of his sons set up a fencing academy. His grandson, Frederick Akbar Mohamed, qualified as a doctor and discovered the dangers of high blood pressure.

Queen Victoria appointed Abdul Karim to teach her Hindustani and in 1894 made him her Indian Secretary with the title of Munshi.

When Britain got involved in the First World War, many in the Indian Army were eager to offer support. By 1918, more than 1 million Indian troops had fought for Britain, more than Canada, Australia and New Zealand. Indian units served on the Western Front, at Gallipoli and in the Middle East. Over 50,000 troops were killed and a further 60,000 wounded. Troops from Indian units won twelve Victoria Crosses, including six on the Western Front. Their Labour units served behind the front lines, constructing roads and transporting ammunition. Their doctors and nurses provided medical support.

Naik Darwin Singh Negi was one of the first South Asians to be awarded a Victoria Cross. In 1914, he was credited with being 'always one of the first to push forward' and retake German trenches under heavy fire. He continued advancing despite an injured arm and two head wounds. Unsurprisingly, he reported sick when the action was over.

Another war hero is Indra Lai Roy, who became a Royal Flying Corps ace. This was an extraordinary achievement because in order to become a pilot, he had to find a way around the regulations that prevented non-nationals from having commissions.

Having overcome that obstacle, he crashed his plane and was sent back to England for retraining. Undeterred, he was back in France in July 1918 and shot down ten planes in less than two weeks. Sadly, he didn't live to see the end of the war and died while he was still a teenager.

South Asians played an even bigger role in the Second World War. While Britain may have felt it was standing alone in Europe, British India was the main base for the British fight against Japan. It provided the largest volunteer army in the war. There was no conscription there and all the 2.5 million troops were volunteers.

Behind the soldiers were a further 8 million auxiliary workers and 5 million working in war industries. Machine guns, shells and aircraft were all manufactured in British India. Indian cotton cloth was used for uniforms and parachutes. Under the Bevin Training Scheme, people from British India were brought to Britain for technical training. The country also provided substantial amounts of money. RAF fighter squadrons began to appear with names like 'Madras' or 'Hyderabad' because their planes were bought by Indian donations.

South Asian forces fought in Europe and North Africa as well as in the Far East. They were with the British Expeditionary Force in France in 1940. They fought in North Africa and then advanced in Italy. At Monte Cassino, the Indian 4th Division suffered over 4,000 casualties. In the Far East, British India provided about 70 per cent of the ground forces. They fought with great courage, winning more than thirty Victoria Crosses and over 1,000 Military Crosses.

In Italy in 1944, Kamal Ram volunteered to take out three German machine gun posts that were holding up the Allied advance. Acting alone, he took out the three posts by sneaking up on them and using his rifle, bayonet and grenades. He was awarded a Victoria Cross for his 'courage, initiative and disregard for personal safety'.

When the war ended there were still not many South Asians living in Britain. The rise in migration was started by a severe labour shortage in Britain. After the Second World War Britain needed more workers to repair the damaged cities, to work in the newly formed NHS and to work in nationalised industries such as the railways. In 1948, the British Nationality Act allowed all Commonwealth citizens to have British passports and the British Government invited Commonwealth migrants to come and work in Britain.

While the British were encouraging people from South Asia to settle in England, the partition of what had been British India caused mass migration and huge suffering. In 1947, Pakistan and India were created, and millions of Hindus and Sikhs found themselves in Muslim-majority Pakistan, while millions of Muslims found themselves in Hindu-majority India. Up to 2 million people died in the process of partition.

Many refugees fled to Britain, headed to England's northern cities and found work in textile factories. Others headed to the Midlands to work in engineering. As the migrants were arriving, many young Brits were leaving to settle in Australia, New Zealand and Canada. British cities rapidly became multicultural, but the process was not peaceful everywhere. Many South Asians experienced severe discrimination and intimidation.

Today, you can see British Asian influence in every supermarket. L.G. Pathak, of curry sauce fame, was born in Gujarat in 1925, but his family moved to Kenya and opened a shop selling Indian sweets. In 1956, L.G. moved to England with only £5 in his pocket. His wife Shanta began selling homemade Indian snacks from her front door, before opening a small shop behind Euston Station. L.G. came up with the idea of making curry pastes so that British families could enjoy the authentic taste of India without the hassle of grinding endless spices. British cookery was transformed.

Rashmi Thakrar of Tilda Rice came to England as a refugee from Uganda. When he died, he wanted to be remembered as a good swimming teacher, rather than an entrepreneur.

Today, people of South Asian heritage are making a huge contribution to every aspect of English commerce, culture and society. While there have been British South Asian footballers in the Premier League, such as Michael Chopra at Newcastle, it is as cricketers that they have made the biggest sporting contribution to England. Nasser Hussain became the first English cricket captain in 1999. Monty Panesar and Abdul Rashid have both bowled for England, Ravi Bopara has batted for them and Moeen Ali is an excellent all-rounder. Isa Guhu became the first British Asian woman to represent England in 2002.

Rapper M.I.A. (real name Mathangi Arulpragasam) was born in London but her parents were Tamil refugees from Sri Lanka. At the cinema, we all think of *Bend it Like Beckham* and stars such as Sir Ben Kingsley and Dev Patel.

6

THE SOMETIMES-WILD WEATHER AND THE WILDLIFE

England is, of course, famous the world over for its beautiful countryside and its often less than beautiful weather.

WHAT'S WRONG WITH THE WEATHER THIS TIME?

In February 1991 the *Evening Standard* claimed that British Rail was blaming its problems on the 'wrong kind of snow', and a new euphemism for a pointless excuse was born. The heavy snow had been widely forecast and British Rail claimed to be well prepared. Unfortunately, the soft, powdery snow was too deep to be cleared by snow ploughs and the snow found its way into electrical circuits, causing chaos.

The weather frequently hits the headlines in the English press. There have been droughts such as the ones in 1975–76, when people were reduced to getting water from standpipes in the streets, and 2022. There have been deadly and destructive floods. In 1928, when the Thames overflowed, fourteen people drowned and 4,000 were made homeless. In 2007, thirteen people died when the UK suffered its wettest May to July since records began.

Frost fairs on the frozen River Thames were an occasional feature of London winters between 1600 and 1814. The Big

Freeze of 1962–63 saw villages cut off, with snow depths of 20ft (over 6m) in some areas.

However, perhaps the most famous of all English weather disasters was, of course, the storm of 1987, which killed eighteen people and destroyed more than 15 million trees. This was a storm best remembered for a BBC weatherman confidently predicting that no hurricane was on the way.

A recent survey confirmed an obsession with talking about the weather was a more important feature of us English than drinking tea. Other surveys suggest what we already know – most of us are happy to talk about the weather and it is a common feature of small talk. Brits, and particularly the English, like to think that we have a stiff upper lip and, in a crisis, we show a Blitz spirit. However, weather is the one thing that we are always allowed to complain about. It is always too hot or too cold, too wet or too dry. We can all agree the weather is never perfect and is always worthy of comment.

Not surprisingly, considering all this, weather idioms are deeply embedded in the English language. We may feel 'under the weather', 'right as rain' or perhaps 'on cloud nine'. At work we can 'brainstorm', 'break the ice', 'be snowed under', 'steal someone's thunder', 'get wind of things' or even 'be a breath of fresh air', but we will still be expected to turn up, 'come hell or high water'.

In our personal lives, we can 'chase rainbows', 'sail close to the wind' or 'throw caution to the wind', 'take rain checks' or 'be on thin ice'. Maybe we should just 'catch some rays'. In the end, the English feel that 'every cloud has a silver lining' and 'there's not a snowball's chance in hell' of finding 'the pot of gold at the end of the rainbow'.

While the Inuit are reputed to have 100 words to describe different forms of snow, the English can knock up a century describing rain. When the heavens open, rain may be coming down in sheets, torrents or buckets. It may be 'chucking it down', pelting, drumming, pouring or even 'pissing down'. Maybe it's just drizzling, spitting, spluttering or sprinkling, or perhaps it's 'getting biblical' or 'raining cats and dogs'. There are many regional variations to describe rain. Cockneys, with their famous rhyming slang, have 'ache and pain' or 'Duke of Spain'. In the West Country, it can be dimpsey, drisk, skewor or henting. In East Anglia, it might be dringey or mothery. In the north-east it could be plash, sea fret, haar or 'siling down', while across the Pennines, in Cumbria, it could be 'hossin down' or 'yukken it doon'. Nobody could really doubt that weather is important to the English.

SO WHY ARE WE ENGLISH SO FASCINATED BY THE WEATHER?

So far, the highest daytime temperature in England was 40.3 Centigrade, recorded at Coningsby in Lincolnshire in July 2022, and the lowest night-time temperature was –26.1, at Newport in Shropshire, in January 1982. The record for most rain in a day goes to Martinstown, in Dorset, where 279mm fell on 19 July 1955, while Seathwaite and Thirlmere in the Lake District hold the records for the most rainfall in two, three and four days. The sunniest month in England was July 1911 with 383.9 hours of sunshine, recorded in Eastbourne – a good year for a summer holiday on the south coast. The highest low-level wind speed was 122mph, recorded at the Needles, on the Isle of Wight in February 2022.

In a global context, there is nothing extreme about these records. There are many countries where 40°C is a normal summer temperature and a low of –26 is not unusual. Even within the UK, England is warmer, has more sun and less wind than other parts of the UK. Technically, England has a temperate climate. The Gulf Stream protects it from winter chills and moderates the summer heat. The only distinctive feature of the English weather is that it is very changeable and perhaps this explains why it is so important to us.

Until the nineteenth century, the weather was often seen as beyond science or rational explanation. Instead, either the will of God or proverbs were used to explain the weather. Do these proverbs work? Sadly, there is no scientific basis to the idea that cows lie down when it is about to rain. 'Red sky at night, shepherd's delight' may be true if it is caused by dirt in the atmosphere trapped by high pressure, but it can also be a sign of increasing moisture in the air and an approaching storm. 'Rain before seven, fine by eleven' is often true because English weather is very changeable, but we do have some longer outbursts of rain. Pinecones opening when the weather is fine is also sort of true as warm, dry weather makes the cones open as they dry out.

And a fascination with England's changeable weather has helped us English to make significant contributions to the development of scientific meteorology. While the origins of a rational explanation of weather may go back to Aristotle and Ancient Greece, the first systematic records in England appeared in the Middle Ages. Between 1337 and 1344, English scholar William Merle wrote the earliest surviving weather diary that we still have. And already by then, English philosopher Roger Bacon had worked out that the summit of a rainbow cannot be more than 42 degrees above the horizon – scientifically true but not much help in predicting the weather.

It was after the Middle Ages that much of the science and equipment of meteorology began to appear. The main stars of the show were probably European, with Gabriel Fahrenheit and Anders Celsius working out how to measure temperature, Evangelista Torricelli developing a mercury barometer and Blaise Pascal and Galileo also making important observations.

For England, Christopher Wren developed a self-emptying rain gauge (as well as designing St Paul's Cathedral and running the Royal Society) and in 1667 Robert Hooke designed an anemometer to measure windspeed. Rear Admiral Francis Beaufort, who developed the Beaufort Scale in 1807 for measuring wind speed, was born in Ireland, although he did serve in the Royal Navy.

Other English contributions came from Edmund Halley (of comet fame), who worked out how trade winds and monsoons were affected by changes in air pressure. Robert Boyle's law determining the links between the volume, pressure and temperature of gases also helped give meteorology a scientific basis and he kept a detailed weather diary for London in 1685. In the late eighteenth century, the Royal Society began to compile weather records.

Pharmacist, amateur meteorologist and Londoner Luke Howard identified and named the different types of clouds in his book *Essay on the Modification of Clouds* in 1803. He invented the categories of cumulus, stratus and cirrus, as well as the compounds of cirrostratus and cirrocumulus. Using Latin names was a marketing masterpiece. In France, Jean Baptiste

Lamark had developed his own categories but chose to label them in French. Latin won out for Luke Howard as the true universal language of the science of the day.

Despite all these advances, the idea of forecasting weather, however, was still being regarded as a joke. In 1854, when an MP suggested that science would allow the house to know the weather in London the following day, he was greeted with laughter. While the MPs laughed, however, Suffolk-born Admiral Robert FitzRoy was already at work creating the Met Office and regular weather forecasts.

FitzRoy had been the captain on HMS *Beagle* and he sailed with world-famous English science legend Charles Darwin around the world on his voyage of exploration. In 1854, he was put in charge of the Meteorological Department of the Board of Trade with the job of establishing a chart depot because better charts would lead to faster trading.

FitzRoy became concerned by the number of shipwrecks around the coast of Britain. Between 1855 and 1860 there were more than 7,000 shipwrecks and thousands of sailors died. FitzRoy believed that if sailors could be warned, lives would be saved. The electric telegraph gave him the technology to gather real-time information about the weather and issue storm warnings. He collected data from weather stations around the country, building an accurate and scientific picture of the weather, and issued storm warnings. His storm warnings began in 1860, and by 1861 he was publishing weather forecasts for the following forty-eight hours in the *Times*.

FitzRoy believed his forecasts were based on science and evidence rather than instinct but his forecasts got a mixed reception. Many people welcomed them. Racegoers at Ascot looked to them for guidance about going and what to wear. Queen Victoria consulted him about conditions for sailing to Osborne House on the Isle of Wight. *Punch* nicknamed him their 'Clerk of the Weather'.

Everybody was happy when the weather was as predicted but when they felt the forecast was inaccurate, they blamed

FitzRoy. Fishermen attacked him when they remained in port and the weather turned out fine and racegoers and fete organisers blamed him for dresses ruined by unexpected rain. To his credit, FitzRoy took to the letters page of the *Times* to apologise and explain the science behind his forecasts. Predictably, MPs even complained about the cost of the extensive use of telegraphs.

Michael Fish became a celebrity and made his name for failing to forecast the 1987 storm; FitzRoy was not so fortunate. The criticism was too much for him and in 1865 he shot himself. It is a sad end for an English visionary, whose achievements still live on today.

While the English like to moan about bad weather, it has, of course, at times been of great assistance to England. The Channel has served as a strong defence against would-be invaders and so has the weather. For instance, in 1588 it was the weather that ultimately defeated the Spanish Armada. Francis Drake may have done his bit to panic the Spanish in Calais, but it was the wind that blew them out into the North Sea and forced them to sail home via the north of Scotland and the west coast of Ireland, where many perished. As commemorative medals proclaimed, 'The winds blew, and they were scattered'.

We English are set to remain fascinated by the weather, now and in the future. More weather information on mobile apps simply means there is more to talk about.

IT'S A WILD LIFE

The weather is the backdrop for the rest of the natural world in England. And what a natural world that is; a world (in many places) of beautiful hills and wide meadows, hedges and fields, rich woods and forest, lovely beaches and rivers, moor and fen, all populated by fascinating animals and colourful birds, insects and butterflies.

We're not going to go into too much detail here on all this, because this is a *Little Book* not *Springwatch* or *Countryfile*, and neither of us is David Attenborough (born in Isleworth, Middlesex). However, here are a few points to consider when thinking about the natural wonders of England.

Nature's National Symbols

Three lions, the red rose, the Tudor rose (red rose with a white rose), and the oak tree are the animals and plants usually associated with England. The English football team have three lions and Tudor roses on their shirts, the rugby team have a red rose and the Royal Navy are fond of marching to 'Hearts of Oak'.

Very large lions did roam Britain in the prehistoric era and may have been around as recently as 13,000 years ago, but they were long gone by the time England arrived on the geopolitical stage. It's easy to see the attraction of the lion as a symbol, representing strength, courage and power for the English, but where did it actually come from?

Henry I was the first English king to use a standing gold lion on a red background and this became two lions when he remarried and adopted a second lion from his new wife's family. Three lions passant-guardant (walking left but facing outwards) were first used by Richard the Lionheart in 1198. He may have chosen a third lion to emphasise his quality as a war leader, but it is more likely to be a reference to his three territories, England, Normandy and Aquitaine.

There is a certain irony that the symbol of England was introduced by Norman kings. Richard I very rarely spent any time in the country. Henry I, although King of England, spoke no English. In French heraldry, a lion passant was called a leopard, only becoming a lion when it stood on its hind legs. Our national symbol, therefore, represents a sort of Anglicisation of Norman kings.

There were some lions in England in the Middle Ages. They were not wild but lived in the royal zoo. The bones of two lions were discovered in the Tower of London. One set of bones dated from the fourteenth century and the other from the fifteenth.

As explored in Chapter 2, the Tudor rose was a brilliant piece of political propaganda, which united the white rose of the House of York with the red rose of the House of Lancaster. The FA have Tudor roses scattered around the three lions on England shirts. The Rugby Football Union (RFU) has instead opted for a red rose. Roses remain a popular symbol for England and a common feature of English gardens.

The final symbol of England, the oak, can be found on the back of some £1 coins. England is represented by a rose but behind the crown is an oak branch and leaves. The oak is England's most common woodland tree. Oak trees can grow to huge sizes. The Bowthorpe Oak in Lincolnshire is hollow and is supposed to have room for twenty people inside it.

In ancient times, oak glades were important to Druids. In more recent times, the strength and longevity of oak meant that it was crucial in building ships (that is, before HMS *Ironside* came along). Oak houses and furniture were also valued. The

Royal Navy has had eight warships called HMS *Royal Oak* and the Royal Oak remains one of the most popular pub names.

Oak trees are fantastic for historical links because they live so long. The Major Oak, Britain's largest oak, is in Sherwood Forest and is thought to be between 800 and 1,000 years old. It was in Sherwood Forest in the time of King John. It is rather less clear whether Robin Hood and his Merry Men were also in the forest.

The Queen Elizabeth's Oak in Greenwich Park, which fell in 1991, is linked not with the late departed Elizabeth but with her Tudor ancestor. The tree dated back to the twelfth century. It was there when Henry VIII and Anne Boleyn danced and when Elizabeth took refreshments within an oak tree. Whether these events took place within this particular tree is, of course, another matter.

Perhaps the most famous oak tree of all is the one in the grounds of Boscobel House, which was used by Charles II to escape the Roundheads after the Battle of Worcester in 1651. Charles was certainly glad to escape and when he became king, he instituted a Royal Oak Day on 29 May to commemorate his escape. Souvenir hunters were picking bark from the oak during Samuel Pepys' lifetime. There is still an oak that is descended from that oak in the grounds of Boscobel House and the National Trust will sell you an oak for your garden descended from the seventeenth-century original.

The oak, the King of the Forest, remains important to the English to this day.

Wild About Flowers

There is, of course, more to the English and flowers than a love of roses. In 2002, the conservation charity Plantlife asked its members to vote on a wildflower for each county. The results are sometimes confusing as the allocated flower has replaced a more traditional one. Yorkshire was allocated the harebell rather than the white rose and Essex got the poppy rather than the cowslip.

Lancashire kept the red rose, although it is not a wild plant, and Nottinghamshire's autumn crocus is not a native plant but an escapee from a medieval monastery.

England Loves its Animals – Mostly

The English see themselves very much as animal lovers, with a deep love of their household pets, and also a concern for the welfare of animals in the wild. Loads of English people, obviously, have pets of various types and sizes, and loads of them are also involved with societies looking after the interests of creatures of various types and size.

In 1824, Britain became the first country in the world to have an animal welfare charity. London vicar Arthur Broome met with twenty-two fellow animal lovers at Old Slaughters Coffee House in London to form the Society for the Protection of Animals. Other members were drawn from across Britain and one of them was William Wilberforce, better known for his campaign to end human slavery. By 1835, the society had encouraged the government to ban bear and bull baiting and by 1844 it had become the Royal Society for the Protection of Cruelty to Animals, thanks to the support of Queen Victoria.

The film *War Horse* shows the terrors faced by animals in the First World War. Horses, mules, donkeys, dogs and pigeons all served in France. The RSPCA went too, and £250,000 was raised and used to pay for four field hospitals for animals. Around 2.5 million animals received care and 80 per cent were fit enough afterwards to return to the front. Field Marshall Douglas Haig thanked the RSPCA for their assistance in the war effort.

The RSPCA is still campaigning. In 2005, it supported the Hunting Act to protect foxes, deer and hares from being hunted with dogs.

In 1889, Britain gained another animal charity, the Society for the Protection of Birds (SPB). Emily Williamson, who was born in Lancaster and then moved to Didsbury, decided that she wanted to campaign against the fashion trend of using feathers and plumes in hats, which was threatening birds such as little egrets and the great crested grebe. She was angry that the men of the British Ornithologists Union did not want to campaign so, with the support of other women, she began the SPB, which became the Royal Society for Protection of Birds in 1904.

The society produced its first report on endangered birds in 1891 and by the 1930s it was beginning to set up nature reserves in Romney Marsh and Dungeness. By 1999, the RSPB had more than 1 million members. Today, more than 500,000 people

participate in its annual Big Garden Birdwatch. The 2022 survey showed the most common birds were sparrows, blue tits, starlings, wood pigeons, blackbirds, robins, goldfinches, great tits, magpies and chaffinches (see photograph p.97). The RSPB has helped to reintroduce birds that had become extinct in the UK, such as the white-tailed eagle, and helped preserve others, such as turtle doves.

A lot of English people are dog lovers. Dog shows began in the nineteenth century and the Kennel Club was formed to standardise rules for these events. Charles Cruft, who grew up in Sussex and London, began the show that now bears his name in 1891 with about 2,500 dogs. The 2022 Crufts Show had more than 16,000 entries.

Mary Tealby founded a Temporary Home for Lost and Starving dogs in Holloway, north London, in 1860. The home moved to Battersea in 1871 and was dealing with over 800 dogs per month. It now reckons it has cared for more than 3 million dogs and cats.

Today, there are also attempts to preserve native animals such as water voles and pine marten. England is also working on reintroducing animals that have become extinct. Wild beavers have been reintroduced in the West Country and wild boar are also making a comeback in the Forest of Dean, Kent, East Sussex, Dorset and Devon.

Of course, in addition to all this worthy work there is also a long history in England of hunting, shooting and killing animals. Fox hunts with their bright red coats used to be regarded as very English.

The world's most famous biologist, Charles Darwin, was born in Shrewsbury in 1809 (on the same day as US President Abraham Lincoln). Darwin had an interesting, varied and at times distinctly surprising career path. He began his studies at Edinburgh University, taking medicine, but left after a year as it was too gruesome. At Cambridge, he studied divinity and formed the Gourmet Club for the purpose of eating unusual animals. Presumably they didn't eat enough to make any actual species extinct.

In 1831 he accepted the job as naturalist on HMS *Beagle*. On his travels around the globe, as well as eating additional unusual creatures, he observed that animals often appeared similar in different continents but also appeared to have adapted to specific environments. Some finches had strong beaks for crushing seeds while others focused on eating insects. The theory of evolution followed, and Darwin went on to upset many of his fellow divinity graduates (in addition to the animal lovers he may have upset with his unusual appetites). Darwin gave all nature lovers a theoretical way of understanding animals and revolutionised how we look at the development of life on the planet.

At Leisure in England's National Parks
In addition to protecting wildlife, the English like to protect the countryside. Well, some of them do.

England has a lot of beautiful countryside, and some of the loveliest areas are national parks. English national parks have special duties that are enshrined in law. They must conserve and even enhance the natural beauty of the area but must also protect the cultural heritage. The areas protected are not all entirely wild. They have been farmed, mined or even, in the case of the Broads, created by man.

While one duty is to preserve, another is to encourage people to enjoy the areas. These laudable aims, of course, are sometimes contradictory. As more hill walkers use the footpaths, the tracks get wider or are sometimes destroyed. The footpaths are repaired to limit the damage, but there is a danger of creating stone highways and destroying the environment. And there is always going to be some tension between the advocates of sports such as mountain biking or off-road driving and those whose focus is more on conservation.

A lot of English poets, such as Cumberland lad Wordsworth, found inspiration in spending time in wild places (all that 'I floated lonely as a cloud, that floats on high o'er vales and hills when all at once I saw a crowd, a host of golden daffodils' bit) and their work publicised the appeal of these spaces and encouraged lots of other aspiring poets to write their own poetry (much of it dire) about the beauties of nature and the countryside.

Landowners were often less keen on sharing the land they kept for hunting, shooting and fishing with the wider public. James Bryce introduced the first Freedom to Roam Bill in 1884. It was rejected by MPs, who favoured the interests of the landowners. Between the wars, as English cities grew and became more crowded, people longed for access to the countryside and fresh air. They began to escape the cities to trespass and came into conflict with gamekeepers.

The mass trespass on Kinder Scout in the Peak District, in 1932, ended with five men in prison but the laws remained unchanged. It was not until after the Second World War in 1949 that the government decided the solution was to create national parks. In 1951, the national parks of the Peak District, Lake District and Dartmoor were begun.

There are now ten national parks spread across the country and each has its distinctive characteristics. For instance, the Lake District has wild fells, but also quarries and slate mines. Strangely, Bassenthwaite Lake is the only lake in the Lake District – the remaining bodies of water are meres, such as Windermere, or waters, such as Derwentwater, and there are a fair few tarns, too.

The Peak District and Yorkshire Dales have the sites of early mills and quarries. And peaks. And dales. Dartmoor has prehistoric remains and tors. And moors.

7

INTERESTING NAMES FOR INTERESTING PLACES

What's in a place name? Quite a lot really.

English place names can be fascinating, historical, weird and funny, sometimes all at the same time. But because the English language has changed over the centuries, you sometimes have to delve a bit deeper to find out what they actually mean.

For instance, Gatwick is today known all over England – and pretty much the world – as a huge, bustling airport. However, if you break the word down, what you get is the old English words '*gat*' and '*wic*'. '*Wic*' is derived from the Roman word for a village (*vicus*) but basically '*gat wic*' means 'goat farm'. Some goats might not want to spend too much time at Gatwick these days, but they were there long before the concrete, tarmac, jets and tourists.

COUNTY CALL

The basic political and administrative structure of England for much of its history has been organised around the counties. The word 'county' itself is interesting since it is linked to the word, yes, 'Count' (as in high-ranking person, not as in 1, 2, 3) and that, in turn, derives from the Latin word *Comes*, meaning companion (of the emperor), which was a term used as a rank in the late Roman Empire.

Some of the county names are just based on the simple principle of adding 'shire' to the name of a major town or city, such as Oxfordshire or Lincolnshire. Sometimes, it's all been a bit abbreviated over the years, so that, for instance, Lancastershire became Lancashire. But some of the county names are also really old and interesting.

We already noted in Chapter 1 the origins of counties such as Essex (nothing to do with sex but a name that is derived from the people, the East Saxons), Sussex (South Saxons) Middlesex (Middle Saxons) and Kent (derived from the name of the pre-Roman and Roman period tribe there, the Cantii). However, there are lots of other interesting ones too. For instance, there are Norfolk and Suffolk. Yes, it's the 'north folk' of East Anglia and below them (geographically), the 'southern folk'. Surrey is a bit similar, in the sense that it comes from old English words for southern and region.

In the west, there is Dorset. The 'set' bit comes from the old English word for settlers and the 'Dor' bit comes from Dorchester, the county town. So, it's 'the people who have settled near Dorchester'.

And then there's Devon. This one's less obvious, but comes from the name of the pre-Roman and Roman period tribe in the area, the Dumnonii, who then formed a post-Roman kingdom, Dumnonia.

Cornwall is a bit the same, in the sense that it contains a pre-Roman and Roman period tribal name, and the 'wall' bit has the same origin as Wales. Somerset is 'the settlers around Somerton'.

Up north, we've got Cumbria, a name that is basically the same as the Welsh name for Wales, *Cymru*, and means 'compatriots'. And, yes, there is Rutland, traditionally England's smallest county and with a character of its own. The 'land' bit of the name is pretty easily understood, but the 'rut' not so much. It's probably not from rutting or ruts but could be from a person's name, Mr Rut or Mr Rota.

BIG PLACES, WITH NAMES
THAT HAVE BIG HISTORIES

England, of course, has some amazing cities, including plenty of lovely old ones, and some interesting new ones too. It's a long time since the end of Roman Britain, but it's fascinating to note that a lot of our major cities were there in the Roman period and have names from that time. And, in fact, a lot of Roman-period names incorporate British names that may even pre-date the Roman occupation of Britain.

So, to start with, we come to England's biggest and most famous city, London. Yep, it's the Houses of Parliament, Buckingham Palace, Tower Bridge, Trafalgar Square, the Thames, Piccadilly, Hyde Park Corner, Harrods, Wembley, the London Underground, the Tower of London, Oxford Street (and all the other locations on the Monopoly Board)! It is one of the world's great cities. London was, in the Roman period, Londinium, which is pretty much just London with a Roman bit added on the end. Nobody is entirely sure what London means, but it's a name that was probably already here when the Romans turned up.

There are quite a lot of names where the Anglo-Saxons took the original name and then put 'chester' or 'caster' or a similar word on the end. 'Chester' is nothing to do with chests, but is an English word, derived from the Latin *castrum* (meaning camp, in the military sense). The Angles and Saxons, coming from lands where big brick-built and stone-built buildings were in short supply, were probably quite impressed by the huge circuits of walls round many Roman-period forts, towns and cities and marked the places out as something special in their names. Sometimes, the names that they gave these places were pretty much unchanged, just with a 'chester' or 'caster' on the end.

Look, for instance, at Doncaster. This was recently made a city in the Platinum Jubilee Civic Honours and already had loads of history before that. Originally, there was a Roman fort and town there called Danum, the same name, pretty much, as the River Don (nothing to do with the mafia, but probably a Celtic word meaning 'water') and so we get Doncaster.

Gloucester got its name in a similar manner. Before the city's beautiful cathedral was built, there was a Roman fort there and then a *colonia* for retired veterans. The name of the place was Glevum, perhaps meaning 'bright'. When the Anglo-Saxons turned up, they put 'caster' on the end and we eventually got Gloucester.

And then there's the great city of Manchester. Before all the nineteenth and twentieth century architecture and Old Trafford and the Etihad, there was a Roman fort called Mamucium or Mancunio. Nobody is entirely sure what the word means but it might be linked to 'mammary' and might mean a hill that looks like a breast. (It is also why Mancunians are called Mancunians.) The Anglo-Saxons added their ending to the Roman-period name and got Mamecestre, which eventually got shortened to Manchester.

Sometimes the names got mangled a bit between the original Roman-period name and the Anglo-Saxon name. So, for example, Lincoln, was Roman-period Lindum, a name that was something to do with lakes or pools. But the Romans turned it into a colony named in honour of the Emperor Domitian, Colonia Domitiana Lindensium. That was all a bit of a mouthful and Domitian fell out of favour pretty quickly after his death, so it was the name Lindum Colonia that eventually was abbreviated to Lincoln.

Similarly, Winchester, with its great cathedral, links to (and statue of) Alfred the Great, and Round Table (the one in Winchester looks like an enormous dart board and is definitely not King Arthur's) was originally Venta Belgarum, the marketplace of a pre-Roman and Roman-era tribe called the Belgae. Out of the 'Venta' element the Anglo-Saxons got 'Wincestre' and then Winchester.

Sometimes the Anglo-Saxons gave up on the original Roman name entirely and just called the place 'caster' or 'chester', as in, for instance, Chester (home of *Hollyoaks* obviously), with its fascinating red sandstone walls. But the Anglo-Saxons, of course, had their own language and were often very happy to use it to come up with new names for the places they came across.

You can't help feeling that when they reached what had been the Roman-period settlement Aquae Sulis, with its amazing hot waters and huge Roman bathing facilities, they didn't think too long and hard before coming up with the new name of Bath. Bath it would still be when Georgian gentlemen and ladies were experiencing its watery pleasures and Bath it still is today.

Similarly, the beautiful town of Wells contains, yes, wells. Again, you feel it can't have taken them long to come up with that one. There is now and, indeed, has been for a long time, the Bishop of Bath and Wells. However, despite the name, this personage is not primarily responsible for water facilities and has, instead, weightier spiritual matters to look after.

The '-ford' city names are often a bit like that as well. Oxford today has a world-famous university, a picturesque city of colleges and museums that has huge numbers of visitors every year and has appeared in many TV and movie productions, including, of course, *Morse* and *Brideshead Revisited*. Yet, to the Anglo-Saxons it was, originally, yes, just a ford where oxen used to spend time.

Hereford, with its huge cathedral and the Hereford *Mappa Mundi*, a fascinating medieval map of the world, was once just a ford where the '*here*' (the army) used to cross. And Bradford, which became such a major force in the Industrial Revolution, the wool capital of the world, and was chosen as the UK City of Culture for 2025, was originally just a broad ford.

And then there are the '-ton' names. These days, we tend to think of towns and farms as very different places to each other, but the word 'town' comes from the Old English word '*tun*', which meant an enclosed space, often a farm. So, Preston, with its impressive industrial and sporting history (Preston North End FC were the first English football champions), was originally the 'farmstead of the priests'.

Brighton is another interesting one. This thriving seaside city (technically Brighton & Hove, as in Brighton & Hove Albion), with its Georgian heritage and modern cultural and social success, was – long before all that – Brighthelmstone, which probably meant the 'tun of Mr Beorthelm'.

'Ham' is another word that appears in a lot of Anglo-Saxon names. It is not, as some people might think, anything to do with pigs or gammon. It basically means 'home', and so 'hamstede' means homestead and 'hampton' means 'home farm'. Although, somewhat confusingly, you can also get 'hamm', which means 'land with water at its sides' in the 'hampton' mix.

So, Northampton, which is not technically a city but is very handy for the M1 and Grand Union Canal, was a 'home farm', whereas Southampton, which is a huge port city from which ships travel across the globe, was a 'farm on land with water around it'. And to save confusion, they added 'North' on the one 'hampton' and 'South' on the other.

'Ham' also often comes added to 'ing'. So, you get '-ingham' on the end of place names. 'Ing' is a bit that was added to a personal name to mean 'the followers, family or entourage of', so the great city of Birmingham, with the Bull Ring, the 2022 Commonwealth Games, and all that huge industrial and commercial heritage, was once the 'home of Mr Beorma's people'. The great city of Nottingham, however, with Nottingham Castle, was once the home not of 'Nott's people', as you might think, but of 'Snot's people'. Yes, Nottingham is mentioned in the Domesday Book in 1086 as Snotingeham.

Inevitably, when the Vikings turned up, they also wanted to have a go at naming places, and some of England's cities still show that Scandinavian influence in their names. Derby has a great industrial heritage (plus Derby County FC, of course, and a statue of Bonnie Prince Charlie because this is about as close to London as he ever got), but a long time ago Derby was just the '*by*' (a Scandinavian word for farmstead or village), where there were deer.

The great city of York, with its impressive cathedral (see overleaf) and walls, started in the Roman period as Eboracum, meaning possibly the 'place of the yew trees'. When the Anglo-

Saxons turned up it became Eoforwic, and when the Vikings came along it became Jorvik.

However, it wasn't only the newcomers to Britain who were producing the city names of the post-Roman era in England. Leeds, once a major mill and industrial town and now again a huge commercial centre with impressive museums, takes its name from the region of Loidis. This is a Celtic name, probably derived from one that meant 'people by the fast-flowing river',

which was used for the area in the post-Roman period and was mentioned in Bede.

Carlisle's name is nothing to do with 'Carl' or 'isles'. The city, with its huge red-stone castle, was in the Roman period Luguvallium, the 'place of Lugwalos' (a Celtic man's name). In the post-Roman period, the Celtic word '*cair*', meaning 'fortified place', was added to the original name. So, the name became Cair Ligualid, then Carleol and eventually Carlisle.

Truro, the UK's southernmost city and Cornwall's county town, has another name of Celtic origin, though, again, nobody is entirely sure of its original meaning.

And some cities were named after their Christian religious function. The lovely city of St Albans is fairly obviously named after St Alban, traditionally known as Britain's first martyr. The beautiful cathedral in the city is dedicated to him and was built near to where he is said to have been executed.

The spectacular Peterborough Cathedral is officially dedicated to Saint Peter, Saint Paul and Saint Andrew, but 'PeterPaulAndrewborough' would be quite a mouthful and instead we just have Peterborough, the 'burgh', or fortified place, of Peter.

AND LITTLER PLACES WITH SOME FUN NAMES

England has a lot of place names. A few of them are quite boring. Dulwich might sound quite dull, but the place itself isn't dull. However, a lot of English place names sound quite jolly, or unusual, or strange.

As you traverse the land, you will often come across places that just sound rather fun. How about Bunny, in Nottinghamshire? Or Diddlebury, in Shropshire? Or how about getting your lips round Chew Magna, in Somerset? Or, for the Harry Potter fans, there's Muggleswick, in Durham.

Having said all that, some of the place names don't, at first sight, exactly seem to act as the best adverts for their towns. Lincolnshire's Spital-in-the-Street doesn't initially sound a great place, but then you realise that 'spital' is actually short for hospital and referred to an old institution in medieval times.

Dorset's Puddletown sounds a bit damp (though maybe fun if you have wellies on) but it's actually a reference to the river next to the town, which is the River Piddle (we will return to this later).

Ugley, in Essex, doesn't sound that attractive at first but the name is not an aesthetic judgement on the village. It is Ugghelea in the Domesday Book and probably contains a man's name – a Mr Ugga, perhaps.

Or how about living in Grotsworth Lane in Cheshire? Or Mucking, another Essex place name?

Rottingdean, in East Sussex, is not a reference to a clergy person past their best, but means instead the 'valley of the family, followers or entourage of someone called Rota' (not rotter). And Rottingdean actually has some rather pretty buildings in it.

Inevitably, though, a lot of the (originally unintentional) humour in English place names comes from the body and bodily functions. West Sussex's Burpham has a jolly name, though it seems to have got jollier over time. In the Domesday Book it was Borham, which does sound, well, boring by contrast. And if you want a more full-bodied name than Burpham, what about Belchford in Lincolnshire? Again, this seems to have got more fun over the centuries. In the Domesday Book it was just Beltesford.

Ticklerton, in Shropshire, sounds a bit, well, tickly. And Bishops Itchington, in Warwickshire, sounds a bit, well, itchy. However, this not a comment on a clergy person having a scratch. Bishops used to own the place and the name means 'farm by the River Itchen' (a pre-Roman name, possibly with a similar origin to that of the Iceni tribe).

And how about the tiny village of Clench, in Wiltshire? What would your reaction be, if you saw a road sign that said Clench?

Of course, there is lots of (fairly) innocent (and obvious) fun to be found in English place names that feature the word 'bottom'. In names, it means the bottom of something (e.g. a valley), not of someone. However, Shakespeare seems to have found fun in the name (see *A Midsummer Night's Dream*), so why shouldn't we?

There is, of course, the famous name Longbottom. It's now better known as a surname (another one for the Harry Potter fans), but was originally a place name in Yorkshire. Waterley Bottom, in Gloucesterhire, sounds a bit watery and a bit of an affliction, but is, in fact, another innocent English place name.

If you are suffering from a waterley bottom, there are places that might sound appropriate to visit. There is, of course, the lovely seaside resort of Bognor Regis in West Sussex. It has royal connections (Regis = 'of the king'), but the 'Bog' in Bognor is not a reference to a royal 'throne' but, in fact, derives from another old English personal name.

Then there is East and West Looe in Cornwall. In the same county we have Flushing. In Devon there is Crapstone. And then, of course, there is the Dorset hamlet of Shitterton. This does seem to be named after what it sounds like, as a reference to some long-ago inhabitants using the local stream for such purposes. Tired of having their place name sign stolen in recent years, the locals eventually had a large rock carved with the name instead.

In similar kind of place name territory, Oxfordshire has Pishill, which apparently was originally named after peas rather than anything else. And in Dorset, we have Piddlehinton. Yes, this is another reference to the River Piddle.

And while there are plenty of humorous bathroom references in English place names, there are also a lot of somewhat amusing names with potential bedroom links. But then this is from a nation who had a seventh-century bishop called Sexwulf (although, if do you want to spoil the fun, you can write it Seaxwulf as well).

Lustleigh, in Devon, sounds like a passionate place, although in reality, it is probably no more so than anywhere else. Titsey, in Surrey, will amuse some. For fans of the US comedy movie, *Meet the Fockers*, there is a Fockerby, in Lincolnshire. The name of Grape Lane in York was originally Grope(****) Lane (with another word attached to Grope, you can Google it if you want). And there is, of course, Penistone in Yorkshire and Cockermouth in Cumbria.

8

THE INDUSTRIAL REVOLUTION, SCIENCE, TRADE AND ALL THAT

With all the beauty of England's countryside and all the pomp and pageant of its royal past, we sometimes forget how good the English have been over the centuries at actually doing things, selling things and making things. In reality, of course, the English have produced some of the world's greatest scientists (Lincolnshire lad, Newton, of course, among them), some of the world's greatest traders (the English and then the British Empire was built on trade as well as guns and the City of London has long been one of the world's major trading centres) and, yes, some of the world's great manufacturers.

Slavery remains a big stain on England's commercial and moral history but, in terms of the development of modern industry and manufacture, England pretty much wrote the book on it (with some help from the rest of Britain). This isn't going to be the most jolly chapter in the book because it contains a lot of serious information about how the world got to be like it is today, but it is important.

INDUSTRIAL POWERHOUSE OF THE WORLD

Between 1750 and 1900 Britain was the first country to have an industrial revolution and became the richest country in the world. Machines replaced skilled craftsmen, human and animal power was replaced by power from coal and later oil, and advances in chemistry and metallurgy saw new materials emerge. It became clear that through trade and industry Britain could get richer and the British could keep enjoying ever-increasing standards of living.

These processes spread across the world as other countries learnt to exploit their resources and joined Britain in seeking perpetual growth. The world is richer because of it and many of its people have a higher standard of living. However, there is no doubt that the benefits of industrialisation have not been shared fairly around the world. It is also clear that global warming and environmental damage are unwanted consequences.

But why did the Industrial Revolution start here in England? It may have been for purely economic reasons. In the eighteenth century, English workers enjoyed comparatively high wages, giving them the wealth to buy more than just food. The wages gave employers an incentive to invent and use machines, rather than pay high wages. The fact that many craftsmen had money spare to spend on, for instance, textiles meant entrepreneurs knew they would get a swift return on their investment. Abundant cheap coal encouraged the move towards steam-powered machines.

It may also have been that there was something special about the English of the period. They were merchants and entrepreneurs, used to trading and investing. There were plenty of non-conformists anxious to show their virtue by working hard and being frugal. There were innovators looking to find practical solutions to making life easier, and there were the gentry, keen for their younger sons to find a way of supporting themselves. The revolution began in England but the Scots, Welsh and Irish also contributed, of course.

SWITCHING ON THE REVOLUTION

Wool had long been a staple of English industry, but it was with cotton that England began the Industrial Revolution. Cotton was easier to mechanise than wool because the threads were more regular and easier to work with than animal fibres. Cotton was also in fashion at the beginning of the eighteenth century as the middle classes began to move away from woollen clothes to lighter, more colourful cotton garments that could be easily laundered.

Raw cotton was imported from the West Indies and distributed to independent families to be spun or woven, before being collected by the merchant for marketing. The work could be done as and when the individual wanted to work, and this fitted around their other jobs.

In a little over fifty years, a series of inventions increased the amount of cotton being produced and as these machines came to rely on water wheels and then steam power, production shifted from a domestic setting to factories.

The process began in 1733 with John Kay's flying shuttle, allowing wider cotton cloth to be more easily woven, which resulted in a shortage of spun cotton. James Hargreaves responded in 1765 with his spinning jenny, allowing a single spinner to produce eight times as much cotton. By 1769, Richard Arkwright had patented a water frame, which improved the quality and strength of the thread produced by a Jenny but it needed to be powered by a water wheel. Consequently, he built a factory on the Derwent at Cromford Mill.

A decade later, Samuel Crompton developed an even faster machine, the mule, which was capable of spinning 1,000 threads at a time but also making finer, stronger threads. The arrival of the Boulton & Watts steam engine in 1781 provided a new power source, which allowed factories to move away from rivers.

Finally, in 1786, Edward Cartwright developed a powered loom and by 1812, all the stages of the cotton-making process had been mechanised and could take place in the same factory. In 1813, there were 2,400 power looms in the country and by the middle of the nineteenth century, about 250,000 of them.

Who Got All the Cash?

Their inventions made history, but the inventors did not necessarily have an easy life. Far from it.

John Kay was born into the business as his father was a woollen manufacturer in Lancashire. (John was born in Bury, whereas Peter Kay of current comedy fame grew up in nearby Bolton!) John was put in charge of the mill at an early age. The flying shuttle was just one of many innovations he made but local weavers were keen to avoid having to pay extra for Kay's patented product. He fled to France and died in poverty.

James Hargreaves was a poor, uneducated Lancashire spinner, who made his invention after his daughter knocked over his spinning wheel. He noticed the spindles kept spinning, even when vertical, and named his machine Jenny after his daughter. When he began to sell his jenny, local spinners drove him out of Lancashire. He had to move to Nottingham, where he opened a small mill and worked hard to earn a modest income and support a large family.

Samuel Crompton was only 5 when his father died, and his mother taught him up to spin and weave. He invented a machine that combined the strengths of both the water frame and the spinning jenny, hence he named it the mule. Too poor to afford a patent, he offered his machine to local manufacturers on the understanding that they would pay him for it.

By 1811, there were more than 4 million mules working around Bolton. That's a lot of mules. However, Crompton was poor and still worked as a spinner. He died in debt; despite being offered £5,000 by Parliament for his contribution to the cotton industry.

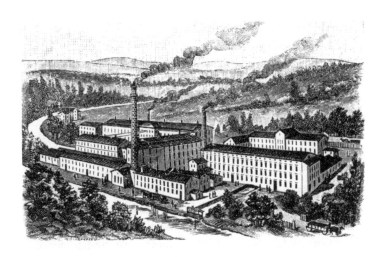

Sir Richard Arkwright was the exception. He was the son of a tailor but began his career making wigs by collecting human hair. He switched from making wigs to making textiles and in 1769 got a patent for his water-powered spinning machine. In 1776, he opened a mill at Cromford, powered by a water wheel, and he built houses to accommodate his workers. He died a wealthy man, owning several mills and a castle.

Factory owners such as Arkwright made their fortunes, but their role was very different from cotton merchants under the domestic system. Factory owners had invested large sums in machinery as well as buildings. They needed a steady supply of completed cotton to sell to cover their costs. Fortunately for them, there was no shortage of demand for cotton cloth.

IRONING OUT THE PROBLEMS

The new textile machines and the steam engines that powered them required huge advances in metallurgy. At the beginning of the eighteenth century, England was importing iron from Sweden. By 1848, Britain was producing more iron than the rest of the world put together and by 1852 it was exporting over 1 million tonnes a year.

This was the amazing work of the ironmasters. While Abraham Darby and his family, of Ironbridge (yes, it has an iron bridge) fame, are the most famous, Henry Cort, Henry Bessemer and many lesser names also made important contributions.

The eighteenth-century iron industry faced a fuel crisis. Smelting iron required charcoal to heat the ore, but there was insufficient charcoal to meet a growing demand for iron. The solution was to use coke as a replacement for charcoal. Britain was fortunate to have a plentiful supply of iron ore, and of coal.

It was Abraham Darby who successfully put the two together at Coalbrookdale in 1709. As a young man, he had spent a lot of time working with brass and he was familiar with using coke in this context. When he founded the Bristol Iron Foundry Company in 1708, he began to experiment with using coke to produce pig iron. Darby was soon producing fine-quality iron pots and pans using the sand-casting techniques he had seen in the brass industry. Darby showed that coke was an economic way of producing iron and his casting techniques showed what was possible.

While many ironmasters followed Darby's breakthrough, others persevered with traditional methods. The science behind Darby's work was not fully understood and variations in the quality of the coal and iron ore used often had unpredictable consequences on the resulting iron. Producing iron was a craft rather than a science, a strenuous form of industrial cookery.

Nevertheless, production of pig iron ramped up. In 1740, Britain was producing 17,330 tonnes per year, by 1796 that was 125,079 tonnes and by 1852, 2.7 million tons. What an increase!

The Darby family showed what could be achieved with cast iron. His son, Abraham Darby II (the family obviously liked the name), cast the cylinders used to make the steam engines designed by Thomas Newcomen. His grandson, Abraham Darby III, built the first iron bridge in 1779.

Other ironmasters followed in their footsteps. Richard Reynold made iron rails in 1767 and John Wilkinson worked out how to bore cast-iron cannon in 1774 – very handy for Britain's military forces, considering the upcoming Napoleonic Wars. Wilkinson also made the cylinders used by James Watt and Matthew Boulton for their steam engine. He overstepped the mark when he decided to build his own copies of their steam engine, however. Watt and Boulton won their court case and then built their own foundry.

Pig iron is brittle and the process of turning it into more malleable wrought iron was both lengthy and labour intensive. The iron needed heating, and the impurities skimmed off and beaten. This was hot work. The solution was found, not by an ironmaster but Henry Cort, a civilian working with the navy in Portsmouth.

His interest in iron came from the navy and, in 1775, he used the money he had earned to buy an ironworks. In 1783, he got a patent for using groove rollers to produce iron bars, rather than hammering them. He got a second patent for a process of puddling iron and removing impurities by stirring it in a reverberatory furnace. The result was a more mechanised way of producing wrought iron.

Sadly, Cort did not benefit from his inventions. His business partner turned out to have invested funds stolen from the navy. Cort had no knowledge of the theft, but he lost his patents nonetheless and went bankrupt.

Other ironmasters made serious money. Richard Crawshay began work as a teenage apprentice at a bar iron warehouse in London. He went on to take over the Cyrfarthfa iron works at Merthyr Tydfil and made a lot of money from supplying ordnance for the Napoleonic Wars. He died as one of Britain's first millionaires, a man whose wealth came from industry rather than land ownership.

The final piece of the metallurgical puzzle was the Bessemer process for turning iron into steel. Henry Bessemer was a polymath, who made a machine to crush sugarcane and another for polishing diamonds. He discovered the process that was named after him in the 1850s.

Although there were numerous teething problems in getting rid of phosphorus and sulphur impurities in his steel, his techniques enabled the manufacture of the armour plating used on Royal Navy warships in the First World War. His contribution was recognised by a knighthood.

'Steel City' had been making cutlery since the Middle Ages. In 1742, Sheffield manufacturer Benjamin Huntsman developed a 'crucible steel process' for creating larger quantities of high-quality steel. And, yes, the process gave its name to the Crucible Theatre, now well known as the venue for the Snooker World Championships.

By the end of the nineteenth century, using the Bessemer process, Sheffield steel was exporting railroad tracks to the USA and producing about 50 per cent of European steel. As a final touch, it was Sheffield chemist Harry Brearly who first made stainless steel in 1913.

DIGGING DEEPER:
THE SEARCH FOR COAL

Coal mining was a dirty and dangerous job, but the ironmasters needed their coke. Coal mining began in open pits, but as demand grew, miners dug deeper, and flooding became a major issue. Teams of men and horses were needed to haul buckets of water out of the mines. Some mines had more than 100 horses. An alternative to animal power was urgently required.

English ingenuity solved the problem. The first steam pump was patented by Thomas Savery in 1698, but it was not sufficiently powerful to raise water from deep mines. Thomas Newcomen invented a more powerful engine and, working with Savery, he built a Newcomen engine at Dudley Castle in Staffordshire in 1712. Newcomen engines spread across Britain, but they were not very powerful. In horsepower they rated a mere 5hp. That is not a lot of horses.

It was the Scot, James Watt, who worked out how to improve Newcomen's engine by adding a separate condenser. Watt made this invention in Scotland in 1765. By 1774, however, he had moved to Birmingham, and he went into partnership with

Englishman Matthew Boulton. Together, they installed Watt engines in coal mines and experimented with them for blowing hot air into blast furnaces. It was Boulton who encouraged Watt to work out how steam engines could be used to power textile factories. Watt's sun and planet gear transformed the pumping action of a Watt engine into rotary motion. At last, the Industrial Revolution had found its major source of power.

Coal production stepped up. By 1800, Britain was using 11 million tonnes of coal per year, by 1830 it was using 22 million tonnes and by 1870 more than 100 million tonnes. Its production was a technical marvel, but there was, sadly, a human cost. Between 1815 and 1829, for instance, over 500 miners died in accidents in Northumberland.

STEAMING INTO THE FUTURE

So, Britain had both coal and iron. It had major ports to bring in raw cotton and to export finished goods. What it needed now was a way of linking everything. This process began with improved roads and canals but ended with Britain as a world leader in the development of railways.

In 1759, Francis Egerton, the 3rd Duke of Bridgewater, decided to build a canal to carry coal from his mines in Worsley directly to the factories springing up in Manchester, 10 miles away. The duke gave James Brindley the job of constructing the canal.

Brindley had little formal education and no experience of building canals. However, he did have a reputation as a resourceful and enterprising engineer. It is amazing that Brindley built the canal without drawings, plans or written calculations. He solved the practical problems of building the canal, the duke recouped the costs of building the canal from increased sales of coal, and the price of coal in Manchester was halved. Everyone was a winner.

The success of the Bridgewater canal inspired other canals. Brindley was responsible for 360 miles of canal building. Other engineers, such as the Scot Thomas Telford, followed in Brindley's footsteps. By the early nineteenth century, canals linked the four main rivers in Britain – the Severn, Mersey, Humber and Thames. They were important for transporting iron and coal, but also for Wedgwood and the pottery industry that was developing in the Midlands.

Railways, like the steam engine, began in the coal mines. The owners of the coal mines built wagonways for horses to transport coal to the nearest canal or navigable river. They needed a gentle gradient that was steep enough for gravity to take the loaded wagons down to the water, but not so steep that brakes failed or the horses were unable to pull the wagons back up the slope. By the end of the eighteenth century, many wagonways began to feature iron rails. It was on these wagonways that the first experiments with steam locomotives took place.

Cornish engineer Richard Trevithick solved the problem of making a steam locomotive that could be used on wagonways. He was no scholar and his teachers thought he was 'slow and obstinate', but he was a talented engineer. Working at the wonderfully named Ding Dong mine in Penzance, he developed the high-pressure steam engine that James Watt had always thought would be too dangerous.

Trevithick's engine was smaller, more powerful and used less coal. It was small enough to be transported in a horse-drawn cart and was just what Cornish tin mine owners were looking for as Cornish mines were a long way away from their coal supplies.

Trevithick continued to tinker with his steam engine and on Christmas Eve 1801 he took seven friends for a ride in the first steam locomotive, which he nicknamed the 'Puffing Devil'. In 1804, he went to Penydarren Ironworks in south Wales and demonstrated that one of his locomotives could haul 10 tonnes of iron and seventy men along a 10-mile trackway. The top speed was 5mph. In 1808, he built a circular track in Euston Square and charged the public 1 shilling for a ride.

As an engineer, Trevithick made some incredible inventions. He developed a steam-powered dredger, a steam-powered boat and a steam-powered threshing machine. However, he was a poor entrepreneur and never made any money from his inventions. His locomotives worked but were too heavy for the cast-iron rails on which they ran. Trevithick died penniless and was buried in an unmarked grave. It was George Stephenson who was to get the credit for being the 'father of the railways'.

George Stephenson had a tough early life. He was born in Northumberland to illiterate parents. As a child he worked at the local mine, picking stones from the coal and driving horses along the wagonway. He paid for his own education at night school. By the age of 18 he could read and write and had a flair for maths. His first wife died, as did their daughter, and his father was blinded in a mining accident.

In 1811 Stephenson got a lucky break. He managed to repair a Newcomen engine at the local mine and the mine owners were so impressed they put him in charge of machinery at all their mines and gave him a salary of £100 per year. By 1814, he had built a steam locomotive named *Blucher*, (the Prussian general who gave Wellington some major assistance at Waterloo) which could haul eight wagons and 30 tonnes of coal at 4mph. *Blucher* became the first locomotive to have flanged wheels to keep it steady on iron rails.

In 1821, when Edward Pease got permission to build a railway between Stockton and Darlington to transport coal to the Tees for shipment to London, Stephenson persuaded Pease to make it a steam railway rather than using horse-drawn wagons. He also persuaded Pease that the railway could carry passengers and other goods as well as coal.

When the line opened in 1825, a crowd of about 10,000 people watched as Stephenson's Locomotion No. 1 pulled more than thirty wagons, some containing coal but others containing passengers, between the two towns. The Stockton to Darlington Railway provided a blueprint for railway development and set the gauge (width between the rails) at 4ft 8½in. However, as the railway operated steam locomotives carrying coal alongside passenger wagons drawn by horses, it is not always accepted as the first railway.

The success of the Stockton to Darlington line made George Stephenson the obvious choice of engineer for building the much larger Liverpool to Manchester Railway. He understood the importance of keeping the track as level as possible. He oversaw the substantial civil engineering achievements of building the line – Sankey Viaduct, the Wapping Tunnel and the cutting at Olive Mount. Even as the railway was being built, there was no agreement about whether the wagons would be drawn by horses, stationary steam engines or steam locomotives.

At the Rainhill Trials in 1829, the *Rocket*, built by George Stephenson and his son Robert came out the winner with a top speed of a massive 30mph. While the opening celebrations were marred by the death of William Huskisson, President of the Board of Trade, who was run over, the railway was mostly a success.

It had been built to carry goods, but it was passenger services that made up more than half of the revenues in the first year. It allowed businessmen in Manchester and Liverpool to meet, do deals and return home the same day.

George Stephenson moved on to develop other railways in the north and Midlands, while his son Robert continued to develop steam trains. Their biggest rival for the title 'father of railways' and someone who is frequently mentioned as a British engineering marvel was Isambard Kingdom Brunel.

Brunel was born in 1806, near Portsmouth, and educated in both France and England. In 1833, the Bristol Railway Committee hired him to survey a railway line between London and Bristol. They were very impressed when he presented his plans in less than three months. The route he proposed was carefully planned to be speedy with few curves or gradients.

However, they were less impressed with his use of a broad gauge of just over 7ft. Broad gauge, although proven to be more stable and efficient for high-speed travel, as well as being cheaper for bulky freight, never caught on. Shareholders were also upset that some of Brunel's civil engineering masterpieces, such as Box Tunnel, the Wharncliffe Viaduct or the Maidenhead Bridge, had been hugely expensive.

Brunel was a visionary. Some of his designs, such as Paddington Station and the Royal Hotel Bath, are still standing. He experimented with an 'atmospheric railway' in south Devon, where trains were moved by stationary steam engines creating a vacuum in a central tube, which then moved the trains along a track. Scientists are still working on developing this idea.

An electric telegraph was installed alongside the Great Western between Paddington and West Drayton to improve communication. Brunel also designed SS *Great Britain*, the first iron, steam-powered but propeller-driven ship to cross the Atlantic.

Even without some of Brunel's more innovative visions, the railways changed Britain. By 1900, all major towns and cities in England were linked by railways. Railway timetables meant that all of England adopted Greenwich Mean Time, or Railway Time. Before that, different towns had had different times.

Railways allowed fresh food to be brought in quickly from the countryside to the towns and cities. They made fish and chips a national dish as fish could be transported easily from the coast. City dwellers began to take day trips to the seaside and travel firms such as Thomas Cook appeared.

Some of England's great shopping chains date from this period. The oldest of the lot, though not a national chain, was Harrods. Charles Harrod began trading as a 25-year-old in London in 1824. Its current building on Brompton Rd has been its base since 1884 and was one of the first shops to have an escalator.

Michael Marks, an émigré from Belarus, began trading in Leeds in 1884. He teamed up with Tom Spencer in 1894. Mark's initial advertising claim was 'Don't ask the price. It's a penny!'

Inflation and a brand premium have (sadly) long since changed that M&S marketing slogan.

John James Sainsbury and Mary Anne Sainsbury began trading in London in 1869. John Lewis started in 1864. Jack Cohen, who founded Tesco, was a comparatively late arrival. It was not until 1919 that he chose to invest the money he had earned during the First World War with the Royal flying Corps into a market stall. He made £1 on his first day's trading (25 per cent profit)!

THE REST

The inventors who drove the Industrial Revolution were mostly practical men with little academic education. They learned how to build steam engines, smelt iron or build machines to make textiles by tinkering with existing machines. However, England has a proud history of science going back to the Enlightenment and the Age of Reason.

Francis Bacon, who worked with both Queen Elizabeth I and James I, might be considered the founder of English science. He argued that old knowledge needed to be tested by experiments and that observation and reasoning would provide new knowledge.

William Harvey explained the circulation of the blood in 1628. His work was based on Bacon's methods.

In 1660, the Royal Society was founded to help scientists get together and share their ideas. Isaac Newton, who wrote the laws of gravity, was president of the Royal Society in 1703.

English science flourished in the nineteenth century as the Industrial Revolution led to more education. Michael Faraday began his scientific career writing a manual on practical chemistry. He will be better remembered for inventing the electric motor and electric dynamo, which have underpinned the twentieth century and look to dominate the search for clean energy in the next century.

The American Thomas Edison is widely considered to have invented the electric light bulb. However, he was working on an idea already explored by the Englishman Joseph Swan. In 1860, Swan built an electric light using a filament of carbonised paper in a glass bulb vacuum. Thomas Edison improved on this idea and in 1883 they combined to form the Edison & Swan United Electric Light Company.

In medicine, Joseph Lister developed antiseptic surgery, cleaning his surgical kit in carbolic acid and operating in a mist of carbolic spray. Many owed their lives to his techniques.

Dr John Snow worked out that cholera in London was spreading through drinking infected water. He solved the problem by removing the handle of an infected pump.

English medical and biological advances continued into the twentieth century, with Rosalind Franklin providing the X-ray photographs that helped to unravel the double helix structure of DNA.

Francis Crick should also get some credit, working alongside American scientist James Watson and New Zealand-born Maurice Wilkins. All three shared the Nobel Prize in 1962.

When considering English contributions to computing, many people of a certain age would opt for Sir Clive Sinclair and his work with the ZX 80 and 81 in popularising home computers. Others might mention Tim Berners-Lee, who has been credited with the idea of the World Wide Web, and Alan Turing, for his work on developing early computers, is another possibility.

However, Ada Lovelace was the first person to try and write a computer code. The computer she designed was never built, but in the 1840s she had the idea that it would be possible to program a machine. She was the daughter of Lord Byron, who was disappointed to have a girl, even though she was clearly very clever.

The British Empire spread across the world and Britain's trading world spread even further to include South and Central America and the Far East. British merchant ships, initially built from wood and powered by sails, by 1900 were constructed of steel and powered by steam and helped spread British ideas around the world. The Scots, Welsh and Irish contributed to this explosion of wealth and ideas, but the bedrock was England.

9

THE ENGLISH: LANGUAGE, LITERATURE AND LYRICS

One of the greatest success stories of England is the language. English is the most spoken language in the world. Approximately 1.3 billion of the 7 billion people in the world speak English, either as their main language or as a second language. This means we have become used to the idea that foreigners will be prepared to speak English. The take-up of other languages in English schools is poor and English tourists abroad tend to expect foreigners to understand them and shout English louder if there is no initial understanding of their words.

The British Empire spread English across the world from North America, the Caribbean, South Africa, India and Australia. International trade spread the language further to countries such as Argentina and Japan. The USA's dominant position in the Free World, Hollywood and the power of the internet have maintained the global position of English.

As we saw in chapter one, the language started in the fifth and sixth centuries when Angles, Saxons and Jutes crossed the North Sea to settle in Britain. The Angles settled in parts of what would become *Englaland* (not 'Engerland!', which is what the football crowds shout) and their language was *Englisc*. About half of the most common words used in modern English can be traced back to Old English. In this context, Old English is not an ale, a man with a threadbare bowler hat, or even an aftershave. It is what we call the language spoken by the early

English. However, pretty much from the beginning, English was collecting influences from elsewhere.

THE CELTS

Celtic words are fairly few and far between in modern English. Tor and crag are two examples. The names of a lot of rivers are still Celtic British. Some experts think the grammar and syntax of English has been affected by the language spoken here before the Angles, Saxons and Jutes arrived.

LATIN AND GREEK

England has had a long association with Latin and about 30 per cent of modern English is derived from Latin. Some of the words were either adopted during the Roman occupation or by the Germanic tribes through contact with the Romans. Many of these words describe simple objects and processes, such as cheese, butter, mile, cook and camp.

The Church used Latin, and words such as preach, candle, wine and bishop were introduced, although not all the language of the Church was in Latin. Gospel was from the Old English 'godspell', or good news. Blessing seems to have come from an Old Germanic word of pagan origin, '*bletsian*'. The meaning seems to have shifted completely, because '*bletsian*' was a blood sacrifice.

Medieval scholars also studied classical Greek. Democracy and tyranny are both originally Greek words.

The Renaissance contributed some scholarly Latin terms to the language, such as aberration, juvenile and pernicious. The scientists of the Industrial Revolution looked back to Latin and Greek to invent new words to describe what they were doing. Vertebra, nucleus, experiment, machinery and formula were some of the words invented.

Some Latin is still used, even though it is not taught in most state schools. Phrases such as '*Carpe Diem*', meaning 'Seize the moment', are relatively well known. Premier League Football clubs such as Everton and Tottenham still have Latin mottos. Everton has '*Nil Satis, Nisi Optimum*' or 'Only the best is good enough'. Spurs has '*Audere est Facere*' or 'To dare is to do'. It is, though, unusual to hear Latin football chants.

The word television is a mixture of Greek, the '*tele*' bit meaning far and the '*vision*' bit meaning, yes, seeing.

THE VIKINGS

As settlers, the Vikings brought words such as cake, from Old Norse '*Kaka*'. Around the house, window comes from Danish '*vind*' and '*auga*', wind and eye. Wrong comes from Old Danish '*vrang*' and ugly comes from Old Norse '*uggligr*'. As raiders, the Vikings left us slaughter, knife and ransack. Probably the most famous donation was berserk, taken from the name of Viking warriors who got into a drunken rage before battles.

NORMAN FRENCH

The Normans introduced about 10,000 words to English. The French fascination with good food made an early appearance with veal, venison, beef, pork, bacon and mutton. The new rulers brought new legal terms such as crime, judge, jury, evidence, justice, slander and bailiff. Military words such as army, navy and soldier were also introduced. Majesty, chivalry and court all showed off Norman power.

When French words were added to the English language, the original Anglo-Saxon words did not all die out and some still exist alongside their Norman replacement in modern English.

Alongside Saxon 'kingly', there are the Norman royal, motherly or maternal, ask or enquire, stench or odour.

We continued to borrow words from the French over the centuries and while most French words we use have been anglicised a little, sometimes we just use a fully French expression, particularly at the table. 'Bon appétit' and 'haute cuisine' are a couple of examples.

ARABIC

A crusade, as in a campaign for political or social change, did not appear until the end of the eighteenth century, but the Crusades, the medieval, armed expeditions launched by Christian Europe, brought contact between the English and Arabs and had an effect on our language. Some of the Arabic influences came via medieval French, Italian and Latin. Others were added later as British trade and influence with North Africa spread.

Arab scholars at the time of the Crusades were more advanced in many areas of science and maths than Christian scholars. The Crusaders brought back the Arabic number system and with it the word zero. The words algebra, alkaline, zenith and nadir are all influenced by Arabic.

Unsurprisingly, the Crusaders also brought back some military terms. Magazine, arsenal, assassin and admiral all derive from Arab words. Carat, as used to describe the weight of a diamond, is based on the weight of a small Arab coin.

Contact with the Arab world brought new food and drink to England. Citrus fruits such as lemons, limes and oranges all took their English names from the Arabic. Tangerines were a later nineteenth-century addition, named after the port of Tangiers, where they were traded. Sugar and coffee were other imports from North Africa. In the game of chess, check, checkmate and rook are all words with Arabic origins.

SPAIN

The Spanish Armada of 1588 brought, yes, 'Armada' into the English language to describe any large body of ships. The period also brought us galleons, flotillas, conquistadors and cargo. A wind can be described as a breeze, which is a borrowing from the Spanish. 'El Dorado' began as a search for a mythical city of gold in the New World, but is now used to refer to any place of huge wealth.

There are many other English words derived from the Spanish, but they have come to us via Spanish influence in central America and American English. Ranch, lasso, stampede, bronco and mustang are all derived from Spanish. Hollywood and US television have helped spread these cowboy words, but have also given us other Spanish words and phrases such as '*Hasta la vista*' or '*Adios amigo*'.

GERMANY

The accession of George I in 1714 gave England a king who spoke German and never mastered the language of his subjects. To confuse matters further, he gave his instructions in French.

German words in English are fairly few. Many, such as pils, pretzel, frankfurter and lager, describe food and drink. Others describe dog breeds, such as poodle, dachshund and rottweiler, and mountaineering has abseil, bergschrund and rucksack.

The world wars brought flak to English from the German for anti-aircraft fire, '*fliegerabwehrkanone*', but it is now also used as a metaphor for a wider range of attacks. We also have blitz, originally used to describe the heavy overnight bombing of London, but now used to describe a concerted effort to deal with something.

Sometimes the English use German to add emphasis to words. If something is 'kaput', the situation is beyond repair rather than simply broken. Other times, German words or expressions are used because there is no English alternative. Hinterland, meaning the area around somewhere, and schadenfreude, meaning taking pleasure in somebody else's pain, are examples of this.

BRITISH INDIA

English is spoken all over the world and so it has borrowed words from all over the world. This being the *Little Book of England*, we can't look individually at every country from which we have borrowed words, but there is one area we must consider.

The experience of British India brought many words back to Blighty (including Blighty). The first reference of soldiers going home to Blighty is from nineteenth-century India rather than the First World War.

As well as curry, we have chutney, kedgeree, mulligatawny and tiffin. In clothing, there are pyjamas, jodhpurs, dungarees and cummerbunds. Items can be 'pukka'. At sea, there are atolls, catamarans and dinghies. A bungalow was a simple building in Bengal for European settlers.

LOVELY LITERATURE

So, once you've got a language, what do you do with it? Obviously, you use it for communicating, but you also use it for books!

The English traditionally don't like to see themselves as intellectuals, they leave that to others. However, in Shakespeare they have one of the most famous playwrights in the world. The English were also heavily involved in the creation of the modern novel and there have been plenty of famous poets. This is their story or, at least, a bit of the story of some of them.

One of the earliest works of English literature, created perhaps in the eighth century, was *Beowulf*. It is an epic poem about how Beowulf rescues the king and then becomes king himself. In the end, he is mortally wounded by a dragon. It's a sort of Old English *Game of Thrones*, but with less nudity. And it's a lot shorter than *Game of Thrones*.

In the fourteenth century, another significant piece of English literature came along – Geoffrey Chaucer's *Canterbury Tales*. It is worth remembering that in the Middle Ages most literate people were clerics, and all books were handwritten. Chaucer worked as a diplomat and courtier for Edward III, Richard II and Henry IV. *The Canterbury Tales* tells the story of a group of pilgrims travelling to Canterbury, who have a story-telling competition. The characters include relatively humble folk such as the miller or the cook, and more affluent people such as the knight, the man of law and the physician, plus some clerics such as the monk and the prioress. It also includes women such as the wife of Bath and her five marriages. The tales are lively and each one has its own approach. They give a fascinating portrait of medieval life.

The development of a printing press in England in 1476, and Tyndale's translation of the Bible in 1526 changed the literary landscape. By 1536, Henry VIII had ensured that there was an English translation of the Bible in every parish, and this helped the spread of literacy.

William Shakespeare was born in Stratford-upon-Avon in 1564. His father John was a glove-maker and held a civic position within the town. Consequently, William was educated at a local grammar school. He married Anne Hathaway in 1582 and moved to London. In 1593, he published his first poem 'Venus and Adonis' and he became a founding member of the Lord Chamberlain's Men, a company of actors. He wrote thirty-eight plays for the company. In 1597 he bought New Place, the largest house in Stratford-upon-Avon (the fruits of fame!) and in 1603, James I became patron of Shakespeare's company, which became The King's Men.

In some senses, this is no more than an English business success story – a man of comparatively humble background, who used his talent to make his money in London by setting up a successful company. He used his profits to invest in property, got royal patronage and died a wealthy man. However, obviously Shakespeare's legacy is much greater than that. His genius was in creating interesting characters. Whether it is the evil Iago in *Othello*, the old rogue Falstaff in *Henry IV*, or the nurse in *Romeo and Juliet*, Shakespeare's plays are full of roles that actors long to play.

The lines are more than 400 years old but still feel relevant. Audiences can still identify with Hamlet's angst or Romeo and Juliet's love, and many of Shakespeare's phrases have been adopted into everyday English. If you have ever felt 'tongue tied' or 'in a pickle', or accused somebody of 'standing on ceremony', you are quoting the bard.

In another sense, Shakespeare also created one of the strongest (and oldest) English brands. His face and name are used to market loads of products. His plays have provided the basis for Hollywood films and musicals such as *West Side Story*. Stratford-upon-Avon has a major heritage industry based on him.

As England emerged from the Civil War, the restoration of Charles II brought new freedoms in the arts. Restoration comedies such as George Etherege's *She Would if She Could* or William Congreve's *Love for Love* were popular (and rather racy) entertainment.

Among the big English literary names of the period were John Milton and Daniel Defoe. John Milton was born in 1608 to wealthy parents and was educated at St Paul's School and Cambridge University. He was an intellectual, who travelled widely across Europe and met, among others, Galileo. He wrote many pamphlets for Cromwell during the Civil War. He is now most famous for his epic poem 'Paradise Lost', published in 1677. While not many people now actually read the poem, words such as debauchery, first used by Milton, are still in common usage.

Daniel Defoe had an interesting life. Born in 1660, he was in London during the Great Plague and the Fire of London. His house was one of only two houses to remain in his neighbourhood after the fire. Unlike Shakespeare, he was no entrepreneur and many of his businesses failed. In 1703, he was put in the pillory for writing a pamphlet. Allegedly, the crowd threw flowers at him rather than stones and drank toasts to him. His 1719 story *Robinson Crusoe* has a claim to be the first English novel.

Other candidates for the first novel include Samuel Richardson's *Pamela, or Virtue Rewarded* (1740), Henry Fielding's *Tom Jones* (1749 – nothing to do with the Welsh singer) or Laurence Sterne's *Tristram Shandy* (1760). John Cleland's *Fanny Hill* was published in 1749. To some extent, it depends on what you are looking for in a novel.

However, among the most significant eighteenth-century English books was Samuel Johnson's *A Dictionary of the*

English Language. Johnson was born in Staffordshire and educated at a local grammar school. He attended Pembroke College Oxford, before moving to London to be a journalist. His dictionary was not the first English dictionary. That honour goes to John Kersey's *New English Dictionary* of 1702. Johnson's achievement was to write a good dictionary with quotes and clear, witty explanations. However, publicity counts, and it was the biography written by James Boswell (Scottish) that really secured Johnson's fame and place in literary history.

Novels really took off in the nineteenth century, with English women writers playing a major part. Jane Austen (1775–1817) led the way. She started writing as a teenager and her most famous offerings are *Pride and Prejudice*, *Mansfield Park* and *Sense and Sensibility*. Her books are mainly about wealthy young women looking for husbands. They are written with a great sense of humour.

The books were originally published anonymously, and it wasn't really until the 1940s that feminist critics took much interest in them. Now, she is almost as famous as Shakespeare, with her books constantly being adapted for film and TV.

The Bronte sisters followed in Jane Austen's footsteps in showing that women could be successful authors. They had roots in various parts. Their father was Irish, while their mother came from Cornwall. The couple met and married in Yorkshire and the Bronte sisters' lives show the grit and determination of which Yorkshire is so proud.

In 1847, Charlotte published *Jane Eyre* and Anne published *Agnes Grey*. Emily's *Wuthering Heights* appeared in 1848. *Jane Eyre* was an instant bestseller, while the other Bronte books took longer to be appreciated. The books are now admired for their detailed descriptions of the harshness of ordinary life in Victorian Yorkshire.

Writer Mary Ann Evans also experienced Victorian male prejudice. Her solution was to write under the name of George Eliot. Her first novel *Adam Bede* was published in 1859 and even Queen Victoria was a fan. Other novels followed, including *Mill on the Floss*, *Silas Marner* and *Middlemarch*.

Charles Dickens was probably the most prolific Victorian author, producing fifteen novels and numerous other short stories and essays. Dickens' story is one of rising from rags to riches through his own hard work and skill. His father was imprisoned for bad debt and the young Dickens worked in a factory. He also received some schooling because he moved to London to work as a journalist. By 1833, he had worked his way up to being Parliamentary journalist for the *Morning Chronicle*. In 1836, he published *Pickwick Papers*, which brought him fame and fortune. *Oliver Twist*, *Great Expectations*, *David Copperfield* and *A Christmas Carol* are among his many books. The appeal of his writing is its ability to stir emotions and readers are able to identify with the characters he created.

Thomas Hardy is another English Victorian novelist, whose work has appeared in films and on TV. He began his professional life as an architect rather than a writer, but with the success of *Far From the Madding Crowd*, he focused on writing. It is

interesting to note that his finest novels are now thought to be his later works, such as *Tess of the D'Urbervilles* and *Jude the Obscure*, although at the time these were seen as shocking. Tastes change but Hardy was a celebrity both now and to his contemporaries.

The nineteenth century ended with a couple of classics, which have been popularised by successful films. In 1894, Rudyard Kipling wrote *The Jungle Book*. Mowgli and his friends began life on paper and without a soundtrack. Around the same time, H.G. Wells imagined an alien invasion in *The War of the Worlds*.

England's most popular poets, the Romantics, also appeared at the beginning of the nineteenth century. P.B. Shelley is best known for his poem 'Ozymandias' but his wife Mary Shelley's novel *Frankenstein* is considerably more famous. As the nineteenth century developed, England's taste in poetry changed. Alfred Lord Tennyson, Rudyard Kipling and Gerald Manley Hopkins were among the stand-out characters.

Early twentieth-century English poetry was, in some senses, dominated by the misery of the First World War and by the work of poets such as Rupert Brookes and Siegfried Sassoon, who illustrated that suffering.

Noel Coward was the most prolific English playwright in the twentieth century, producing over fifty plays. His first, *The Last Chapter*, was in 1917 and his final play was *Star Quality* in 1967.

John Osborne kick-started a new wave of theatre with *Look Back in Anger* in 1956. He was the first of the so-called Angry Young Men.

Harold Pinter followed in Osborne's footsteps. In 2005, he was awarded the Nobel Prize for Literature. Plays such as *The Caretaker* and *No Man's Land* were said to 'uncover the precipice under everyday prattle and force entry into oppression's closed rooms'.

Tom Stoppard was born in Czechoslovakia but emigrated as a child to avoid the Nazis. He has won numerous awards for plays such as his take on Hamlet, *Rosencrantz and Guildenstern Are*

Dead, and *Travesties*. The land of Shakespeare is still producing new playwrights.

Literature has played an important part in raising the matter of women's rights. Virginia Woolf brought a women's perspective to modernising the English novel with books such as *Mrs Dalloway* and *To the Lighthouse*. Caryl Churchill has flown the flag for women and won awards with plays such as *Top Girls*.

D.H. Lawrence is perhaps now best known for his book *Lady Chatterley's Lover*. He published the book privately in 1928 and it was not until Penguin won an obscenity trial in London in 1960 that it could be published. There have now been numerous film and TV adaptations. However, some readers prefer Lawrence's autobiographical *Sons and Lovers* or *Women in Love*.

George Orwell is famous for his books *Animal Farm* and *1984*.

We have now run out of space for our brief look at some of the greats of English literature. Today's impressive crop of English writers includes many who reflect the more diverse nature of England today, with the likes of Zadie Smith, Hilary Mantel, Kazuo Ishiguro and Monica Ali. In 2019, Bernardine Evaristo became joint winner of the Booker Prize – the first woman with black heritage to do so.

LUSCIOUS LYRICS

As well as having some of the best books in the world, England has some impressive achievements in other areas of culture too. We have, for instance, some great artists, such as J.M.W. Turner (born in Covent Garden). ." To And we also have many great actors and famous directors on both stage and screen.

However, globally, we are perhaps best known for our music. And while many people do listen to Purcell, Benjamin Britten and Vaughan Williams, what we really mean here is, yes, pop and rock. So, this is where we take a brief, slightly random journey through a bunch of English singers and bands.

The 1960s

While the earliest existent English lyrics are from the thirteenth century and Cliff Richard's career started in the 1950s, it was in the 1960s that English pop music really kicked off. The Beatles led, with success on both sides of the Atlantic. Mick Jagger and those Stones released the first of their thirty studio albums in 1964. Eric Clapton began his career with the Yardbirds and then Cream in the 1960s. Status Quo had their first hit with 'Matchstick Men' in 1968 and are still going.

The 1970s

The 1970s saw an explosion of new types of music in England. There was folk rock, psychedelic rock, glam rock, progressive rock, hard rock, heavy metal, punk and ska. Young people were spoilt for choice.

Elton John began his extraordinary career with the hit 'Your Song' in 1970. He is still performing and is well known for his outrageous outfits featuring bright colours, flowers, feathers and fancy glasses. His music is not bad either, with 'Candle in the Wind' being his most successful single.

Freddie Mercury (of South Asian heritage and born in Zanzibar) could rival Elton as the most glamorous English star, but sadly his career was more short-lived. David Bowie, with his Ziggy Stardust persona (one of many), completes the glam rock trio.

Leading the way in psychedelic rock were Pink Floyd, with their 1973 classic, 'Dark Side of the Moon'. Genesis had success under the progressive rock banner and went on to produce a series of hits in the 1980s and 1990s with albums such as 'Invisible Touch'.

Led Zeppelin began life in the 1960s, but it was with their album *Led Zeppelin IV* in 1971 and 'Stairway to Heaven' that they really hit the big time.

Ska bands Madness and The Specials began experimenting with Reggae-based music. They were formed in England, although neither is exclusively English, and Madness are still attracting large crowds.

The Sex Pistols started punk rock, and with 'God Save the Queen' they both shocked the nation and influenced youth culture. Groups such as Siouxsie and the Banshees followed in their footsteps.

The 1980s

The 1980s saw a series of bands whose music had the energy of punk rock but was less aggressive. Electronic keyboards and drum machines began to feature more prominently. Bands such as The Human League, Bananarama and Spandau Ballet became hugely popular and still are. Perhaps the most famous of the New Wave bands were Duran Duran, who had fourteen top ten singles. Their ground-breaking videos shown on MTV helped to promote them.

The 1990s

Boy bands, girl groups and Britpop were the key features of the 1990s. Take That were hugely successful with a dozen No. 1 singles and eight No. 1 albums in the UK. East 17 had a rather tougher image.

The Spice Girls were formed by Bob and Chris Heart, who decided to create a girl group to rival the popular boy bands. Their debut single, 'Wannabe' reached No. 1 and their album *Spice* sold more than 23 million copies. The Spice Girls only made three albums, but their 'girl power' message made them role models for young women both in England and around the world.

Britpop was invented by the *New Musical Express* to label a group of bands that saw themselves as following in the footsteps of legends such as The Beatles and the Stones. The key bands involved, Oasis, Pulp and Blur, often preferred to emphasise their own talents rather than celebrate the collective good. It produced some impressive music. For Pulp, there was Jarvis Cocker's hit, 'Common People'. Blur had success with their 1994 album *Parklife* and Oasis came up with the famous *(What's the Story) Morning Glory?*.

The Twenty-First Century

England's reputation for producing great music has continued into the twenty-first century. We have great singer-songwriters such as Ed Sheeran, Adele, James Blunt and the now sadly deceased Amy Winehouse. There are also new influences from rap music and grime with Stormzee.

10

THE ENGLISH AND FOOD

We love our food in England, but traditionally we have left fancy cooking to other nations. However, there have long been some delicious mouthfuls on the menu in this country.

BREAKFAST

W. Somerset Maugham suggested that to eat well in this country you should simply choose breakfast for every meal. The full English breakfast, featuring all, or a selection from bacon, egg, sausage, black pudding, tomatoes, mushrooms and baked beans, is a relatively recent tradition. In the early Middle Ages, breakfast was only for children and pregnant women. For everybody else, the day began on an empty stomach, and it was not until mid or late morning that the fast was broken. This was an age dominated by religion.

By the late Middle Ages, landowners had decided that going hunting on an empty stomach was no fun and a large pre-hunt breakfast added to both the fun and the spectacle. A hunting breakfast did sometimes feature sausages and bacon, but halibut, pheasant, pigeon and lambs' kidneys were also common. It was an opportunity to flaunt your wealth.

By the end of the nineteenth century, wealthy industrialists and an aspiring middle class decided that a cooked breakfast was the way to start the day. Bacon and eggs were common ingredients but tomatoes, although available, were yet to find favour in England. Cooks needed to be well organised to get bacon, eggs and toast ready at the same time, particularly if the master required porridge as well. Toast was toasted over an open fire and was more an afternoon snack or supper dish.

The twentieth century brought electric toasters and domestic electricity. By the 1950s, a full English could also be enjoyed by the working class, either prepared at home or taken at a café. It was a national dish. Although at home its popularity has declined, a full English takes pride of place on many British café, restaurant and hotel menus today.

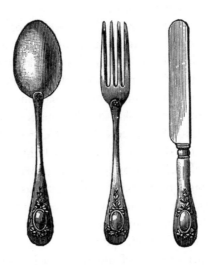

SOME FAVOURITE BITES

When people think of English food, obviously many immediately think of roast beef and Yorkshire pudding or fish and chips, or perhaps a recent addition to menus here – yes, chicken tikka masala.

Roast beef has long been popular in England. The Normans gave us the word beef (in French, *boeuf*). When looked after by the Saxons on farms, the animals were cows or oxen, but on the table their meat was beef. Beef was the most popular meat in the twelfth-century English cookbook, *Forme of Cury*. For the nobility, banquets of roast beef were an opportunity to show off.

The English became famous for their love of beef. At the Tower of London, the Yeoman Warders in their red uniforms are known as Beefeaters. This may be because, as the king's bodyguards, they ate beef leftovers from the royal household. However, it may also come from the French '*buffetier*', meaning a food taster. English kings were not short of enemies and worried about being poisoned.

By the eighteenth century, the French were happy to nickname the English '*les rosbifs*' and in London there were beefsteak clubs such as The Sublime Society of Beefsteaks, with the motto of 'Beef and Liberty'. Simple roast beef had come to represent the British values of manliness and plain common sense.

The eighteenth century also saw the emergence of Yorkshire pudding in Hannah Glasse's *Art of Cookery Made Plain and Simple*. Yorkshire pudding was a lighter and crispier development of earlier dripping puddings, which were made from the drippings from beef as it was spit roasted in front of a fire. Originally, these puddings were served as an appetiser with gravy to fill diners up before the beef arrived, rather than an accompaniment to the beef, as it is now.

Sunday dinner – roast beef and Yorkshire pudding – remains popular, but a survey of soldiers in France during the First World War showed that the meal they longed for when they got home was roast chicken rather than beef. It now faces strong competition from chicken or vegetarian options. Moreover, if you want your beef roasted over an open wood fire rather than put in a hot oven, you are likely to be disappointed.

Fish and chips are another firm English favourite. Fried fish with a coating of flour or batter was first introduced to England by Sephardic Jews in the seventeenth century. Cooking is forbidden on the Jewish Sabbath, so Portuguese Jews fried fish in flour on a Friday afternoon to help preserve the fish and it was eaten cold on the Sabbath. When Portugal became part of Spain, at the end of the fifteenth century, the Inquisition was introduced, and many Jews left the country. Portugal and Spain's loss was our gain. By the end of the eighteenth century, a British cookbook talks about 'the Jews' way of preserving fish' and by the 1830s, Dickens is writing about 'fried fish warehouses'.

Although potatoes arrived in England in the sixteenth century, it is not until 1817 that William Kitchiner (appropriate name) produced a recipe for chips in his *The Cook's Oracle*. By the 1860s, chip shops appeared in Dickens' books.

It remains unclear whether frying potatoes to produce chips is an English invention or was imported from Belgium. Nor is it clear who first decided to combine fish and chips and open a shop to sell them. It may have been a young Jewish man, Joseph Malin, who established a London shop in the 1860s, which lasted more than a century. Or it may have been businessman John Lees, who sold fish and chips at Mossley Market in Oldham, also in the 1860s.

An important factor in the development of fish and chips as an English staple was the growth of the railways and the introduction of industrial-scale, steam-powered trawlers. These provided the growing industrialised cities of England with a plentiful supply of cheap fish.

By the 1930s, there were 35,000 fish and chip shops and George Orwell credited them with saving England from revolution by feeding the poor. Fish and chips were not rationed in either of the world wars because the government feared such rationing would leave many starving and harm the war effort. On D-Day, during the Second World War, British soldiers identified themselves by shouting 'Fish!' and waiting for the response, 'Chips!'

Sadly, fish is no longer cheap, and shops are no longer allowed to serve it wrapped in newspaper. However, there remain 10,000 chip shops and according to the industry, people eat, on average, six portions of fish and chips each per year.

In 2001, the Foreign Secretary Robin Cook declared that chicken tikka masala was Britain's national dish. It is certainly widely available in restaurants in England and, as a ready meal, in most supermarkets. Not everybody agrees on where the dish came from, but it is often said that it was developed in a Glasgow curry house when one customer thought his chicken tikka was too dry and wanted a sauce. The chef mixed some tomato soup and cream with some spices and chicken tikka masala was born.

10 OTHER DELICIOUS ENGLISH DISHES

There is no definitive list of favourite English dishes, and it is difficult to decide which others best sum up English tastes in food. This is a selection of possibilities.

Savoury Dishes

SAUSAGES AND MASH
There are many regional varieties of sausage – Cumberland sausages: the long meaty ones; Lincolnshire sausages: with sage and thyme; Manchester sausages: flavoured with cloves, ginger, nutmeg and mace. They can be served with mashed potatoes or cooked in Yorkshire pudding to make toad-in-the-hole.

BUBBLE AND SQUEAK
A dish from the frugal school of English cookery. Dating back to the beginning of the nineteenth century, it was simply a way of frying up meat and vegetables from a Sunday roast dinner. Now, it is based on potatoes and vegetables rather than meat.

STEAK AND KIDNEY PUDDING

Steak and kidney pudding uses suet pastry and is steamed, while steak and kidney pie is baked using short crust pastry. Savoury meat puddings date from Georgian times.

SHEPHERD'S PIE

A modern English staple but a source of much confusion. Shepherd's pie is based on lamb while cottage pie is based on beef, but today, the terms seem often to be used interchangeably. The origin of the dish may be English, but the name seems to have been first recorded by a Scot, and the Irish, with a long-standing taste for potatoes, may also have a claim.

PLOUGHMAN'S LUNCH

Bread, cheese and ale was the meal of choice for agricultural labourers in the Middle Ages. The term 'ploughman's lunch' first appeared in the nineteenth century, and it was promoted after the Second World War by the Milk Marketing Board to increase sales of cheese. (English cheese is, of course, not just Cheddar. There are many varieties, ranging from Stilton, Red Leicester, Cheshire, Double Gloucester and Wensleydale to Cornish Yarg or Somerset Brie.)

Sweet Dishes

SPOTTED DICK

Nobody knows where the name came from. The suggestion that dick was some sort of Old English word for pudding is one of the more polite versions. It is a suet pudding with currants to add sweetness and a rather questionable name. Very English.

TRIFLE

How strange – a single word that describes both something of little value and a traditional eighteenth-century English dessert. The dish was a way of using up old cake by soaking it in alcohol and then adding fruit or jam and topping with custard and cream.

Banoffee Pie

A modern addition, invented by Nigel Mackenzie in the 1970s when he found his restaurant short of a dessert. A combination of bananas, caramel and cream on a crushed biscuit base.

Mince Pies and Christmas Pudding

As the name suggests, mince pies began in the Middle Ages, originally being made from animal products. Only in the nineteenth century, as dried fruit became cheaper and more available, were the original key ingredients replaced. Plum pudding made a similar journey, starting as a pottage or soup with meat and dried fruits, served as a first course. The Victorians took away the meat and it became a solid pudding.

Bread and Butter Pudding

This is another recipe from the frugal school of English catering; a way of using up bread that was about to go stale by buttering it and adding raisins and custard. This was first recorded in the eighteenth century.

ENGLISH FOOD:
A TASTE OF HISTORY

Of course, in a land with as much history as England there is bound to be some fascinating food history. And this is where we serve some up.

The Romans

The Romans brought wheat corn from Africa and brewer's yeast to make leavened bread. Bread ovens were features of Roman forts and towns. Romans introduced food in England with strange new flavours, the most powerful of which was *garum*, a fermented fish sauce. Herbs such as mint, coriander, rosemary, radish and garlic were also cultivated. Many vegetables that we still use today, such as turnips, cabbages, celery and onions, first appeared at this stage and vineyards were established.

The Saxons and Vikings

A Saxon word for lord was '*hlaford*' or 'loaf keeper', while for the lady there was the word '*hlarbadigin*' or 'bread kneader'. In fact, it was much riskier to bake bread in wooden Saxon houses than in the stone dwellings of the Romans.

Most Saxons relied on pigs for meat. A bacon sandwich was possible for many, while the poor relied on porridge and vegetable stews washed down with ale. The elite favoured beef. Vikings added more flavour as they were experts in preserving meat and fish by smoking and drying it. Yarmouth bloaters (smoked herring) and York ham (smoked with oak chips) may be linked to Viking settlement in those areas.

The Normans

The Norman Conquest brought a new ruling class with new tastes in food, although for the conquered Saxons there was comparatively little change in food at the time. For the Normans, it was all about the meat.

Rabbits, known as coneys, were introduced and farmed in large warrens. There is a medieval recipe for rabbit in almond milk. Pigeons were kept in dovecotes for pigeon pie. Venison was very popular, and Norman hunting rights were enshrined in strict Forest Laws to prevent poaching. Swans, all owned by the king, peacocks, beaver tails and even badgers appeared on the table. In this meat feast, there was only one exception – horses were not to be eaten in medieval England.

Fish were very popular. Freshwater fish such as carp, tench and pike were all kept in fishponds known as stews. These were very popular in monasteries, where the monks needed a supply of fresh fish for fasting days, when eating meat was forbidden. Fish was valued and expensive. A large pike was worth about the same as two pigs. The stone for Ely Cathedral was paid for by sending the supplier 8,000 eels per year. It is unknown how many years the arrangement lasted.

The Middle Ages

Seafood was important at this time, and cod and herring were popular and readily available by the coast. They were preserved either by smoking or salting. Red herrings were smoked herrings in which the smoke had turned the flesh red. They were used to train hunting dogs and, once the dogs were trained, they were used to test them to see if they could still follow the faint smell of the animals being hunted or were put off by the strong smell of the red herrings.

Whales, seals and porpoises also turned up on medieval tables. There was very little that the medieval man was not prepared to eat.

The Crusades spiced up English cooking. Pepper, saffron and ginger were already popular in medieval England but the Crusaders brought home cinnamon, cloves, nutmeg and sugar.

Spices were hugely expensive. Loaf sugar could cost between 1 and 2 shillings when, by comparison, a servant's yearly wage was 4 shillings. Edward I spent £1,600 per year on spices at a time when building an entire castle cost £15,000.

Despite the costs, medieval cooks used spices in large quantities to counter the salt and smoking that had already been used to preserve meat and fish. We must have been a wealthy country.

Medieval English food was quite sophisticated and had strong flavours. The tradition of pairing mint sauce with lamb was already established; venison was paired with sugar and cinnamon; capons, male chickens, were packed with dried fruit and lemon rind. Sweet and sour sauces were used to flavour freshwater fish.

By the end of the Middle Ages, landowners were enjoying very fancy food. Banquets had several courses, but each course contained a variety of sweet and savoury dishes. Diners were not expected to eat everything but to be selective – a sort of fancy buffet. Below is the first of four courses from an upper-class meal:

FIRST COURSE
Brawn of boar with mustard.
Pottage of herbs, spice and wine.
Beef, mutton, pheasant and swan with a sauce made from chopped liver and entrails boiled with blood, bread, wine, vinegar, pepper, cloves and ginger.
Capon, pork, baked venison, meat fritter and pork, eggs, currants and spices boiled in a bladder and served with a sauce.

The Tudors
The Tudors and Stuarts continued the theme of rich English cooking and by the end of seventeenth century, the English had established a reputation as the gluttons of Europe; a reputation which, to some extent, is still with us.

Salads and raw vegetables were not for the English. While Catherine of Aragon loved salad and Henry had a vegetable garden built to provide her with fresh produce, English cookbooks saw salads as dangerous and potentially poisonous – definitely to be avoided.

New ingredients from the Americas got a muted reception. Henry VIII liked sweet potatoes, but normal potatoes did not at first catch on. Their shape led to them being recommended as a male aphrodisiac, just as kidney beans were supposed to be beneficial for those with kidney stones at the time. Tomatoes were popular in Spain and Italy but did not catch on in England.

Sugar, however, was an instant hit. Elizabeth's black teeth showed her enthusiasm for it. Sugar would make tea, coffee and chocolate both palatable and popular.

As well as rich food, the English liked their drink (another reputation still with us!). Ale was drunk by most because it was cleaner and safer than water. It was dark and bitter and made with a range of ingredients, although not hops. Beer with hops was introduced from the Low Countries in the seventeenth century. Ale was drunk by both men and women. Elizabeth I started her day with ale for breakfast and maids of honour at Henry's court received 8 pints of ale per day, while his royal court consumed 600,000 pints of ale per year. That's quite a bar bill.

The Tudor army refused to fight without ale. When Henry VIII sent his army to Spain to help King Ferdinand, they mutinied and came home when the ale ran out. In 1542, the Duke of Norfolk refused to advance into Scotland until his army's ale had arrived and he withdrew after four days when the ale ran out. The army did indeed march on its stomach.

Henry VIII's Dissolution of the Monasteries led to the creation of ale houses and the start of the great English pub. In the Middle Ages, the Church had provided food and drink for travellers and locals; now it became a commercial proposition for entrepreneurs.

Wine was not initially considered a suitable alternative to ale for most. It was more expensive than ale, although it was widely available. By Elizabethan times, about eighty types of wine were drunk, drawn from all over Europe. French wine was popular but there was also wine from Italy, Germany and Spain. The Tudors were the first to taste Spanish sherry, which was, of course, to become a favourite of middle-class England.

The Stuarts and the Commonwealth

It is said that in 1647, Balliol College student Nathaniel Conopios was the first to brew coffee in England. It seems that it was migrants who introduced coffee shops to England.

Oliver Cromwell opened England to Jewish refugees who were fleeing persecution. In Oxford, a Jewish man called Jacob established a coffee shop in 1650 and England's love of coffee began. By 1663, there were eighty-two coffee houses in London. It appeared modern and progressive to a new urban elite.

Coffee was originally drunk black, but it was not long before the English started to add milk, sugar and a whole variety of spices. Each coffee house had its own varieties and specialties. The Grecian was for the intelligentsia, the Bedford for theatre lovers, Waghorn's for political discussion.

Coffee was marketed as a health drink, 'preventing drowsiness and making one fit for business'. Coffee houses were places for men to meet and discuss things. William Harvey, who discovered how the heart worked, left £56 to the London College of Physicians to fund a monthly coffee meeting.

The coffee house craze was short-lived. Free speech may be an English tradition, but this was too much freedom for the government, and in 1673 it attempted to close coffee houses. While inns and tea houses were places for mixed company, coffee houses were an all-male preserve.

By the late eighteenth century, coffee drinking had spread to the domestic environment and coffee houses had been replaced by ale houses, tea houses and gentlemen's clubs. Good coffee became hard to find in England until the 1980s.

England's favourite drink – tea – also appeared here in the late seventeenth century. Charles II's wife, Catherine of Braganza, popularised the drinking of Chinese tea among the middle classes.

Tea was extremely expensive. In 1707, Thomas Twining was selling his gunpowder green tea for £800 per pound. Most of this was down to government tax, and eighteenth-century smugglers saw this as a business opportunity. Tea was light and easy to smuggle, could be bulked up by adding leaves from other plants and could be sold for high prices to people eager to get a taste of this middle-class habit. In 1784, William Pitt the Younger realised he was fighting a losing battle and reduced the tax. Tea was now affordable, and the smugglers went out of business.

Merchants realised that sourcing tea from China was difficult and expensive. So, in the nineteenth century, British merchants started growing tea in India. Keeping production within the Empire made economic sense.

Indian tea had a stronger flavour than Chinese tea, and so the English tended to add milk to it, partly to make it more acceptable to English tastes of the time. Tea, like coffee, was advertised as a healthy drink, although not everybody agreed.

As coffee houses faded, tea houses replaced them. Tea was easy to brew, requiring nothing more than a kettle, and many families kept a brew on all day. The poor could afford it by reusing dried leaves or using additives. Ladies took the opportunity to socialise over afternoon tea and by the end of the nineteenth century, office workers and shoppers would be able have tea and cakes in urban tea shops such as Lyon's in London.

While European countries drank coffee, the English were defined by their love of tea. It could be drunk at home, in a work canteen or restaurant. Shared by both sexes and all social classes, it came to unite and define the English.

The Aztecs liked to enjoy a cold chocolate drink. However, the English version of chocolate needed the addition of both sugar and milk to become part of our national diet.

It was Spanish friars who first added sugar to chocolate. England acquired chocolate in the seventeenth century when Cromwell's troops captured Jamaica from the Spanish and took over a cacao plantation.

Hot chocolate spread amongst the seventeenth-century middle classes, who were keen to try another new health drink. Samuel Pepys liked it, as did Charles II's doctor, Mr Stubbe. Queen Anne's physician Hans Sloane first decided to mix milk with chocolate, a secret that was eventually passed on to the Cadbury brothers in 1824.The Cadburys made a commercial success of cocoa and Stubbe also became very wealthy. England's love affair with milk chocolate had begun.

The Georgians

Pehr Kalm, a Swedish visitor to England in 1748, observed that Englishmen did not go far beyond roast beef and plum pudding in their cookery. His assessment would have seemed more like a compliment than a criticism to many Georgians. The Georgian Court enjoyed roast meat and comparatively plain food. It was seen as more of a virtue than fancy French cookery.

Georgian England was a land of plenty. The agricultural revolution meant more food was being produced, enough to feed a growing population. As the Puritan influence declined, the tendency to overindulge increased. Obesity and gout were common health problems.

The sandwich, still a key feature of the English diet today, was a common-sense Georgian innovation. John Montagu, 4th Earl of Sandwich, asked his servant to prepare two pieces of bread and some sliced meat, so that he could have a snack. Whether he was forced to snack one-handed because he was working so hard at the Admiralty or too busy playing cards at a club is a matter of dispute. However, there is no doubting the importance of the sandwich to English life.

As Georgian cookery moved away from spices, many of our favourite English dishes emerged. Ice cream became popular, with ice houses a feature of many wealthy Georgian homes. Jelly was also in demand. Wild strawberries were replaced with larger, farmed strawberries and tomatoes and the new wonder vegetable cauliflower started to appear in recipes. Hannah Glasse mentions fried potatoes in her cookbook, indicating that potatoes were finally becoming accepted. Hannah does mention at least one dish that had plenty of spices. An early recipe for an Indian curry shows the growing importance of India in cookery here.

The Victorians

For wealthy Victorians and Edwardians, food was a chance to show off wealth and status. Tables contained more food than could possibly be eaten and leftovers were distributed to servants and staff. Prince Edward regularly had a cooked breakfast and found room for a dozen courses at lunch and dinner.

The fashion in food moved away from plain Georgian recipes to fancy French sauces and many wealthy households had a French chef. These were sometimes unimpressed by English

tastes. The Duke of Wellington's French chef left his employ when he realised the duke always poured vinegar over his carefully prepared dishes. Books on etiquette at the dinner table became bestsellers.

Alongside the taste for fine French cuisine, the Victorians also started some English bad habits. The tendency to boil vegetables until they became tasteless can be found in Mrs Beeton's nineteenth-century books and Elizabeth Arden in her *Modern Cookery*, published in the nineteenth century, advised against using garlic.

Industrialisation and urbanisation also contributed to the idea that the English didn't know how to cook. The urban poor had few facilities to cook hot food and became dependent on cheap street food such as baked potatoes and, later, chips. The quality of bread, meat pies and sausages varied a lot, with a wide range of additives, some toxic, being used in food.

Convenience food also appeared in the nineteenth century. Peter Durand set up a canning business in London in 1810, mechanising a French idea for food preservation. For the British Army and Royal Navy canned food was a useful supplement to the usual diet of salt beef and biscuits. Commercially, it was condensed milk that convinced the English that tinned food was a good idea and it was tinned food that would help Britain to feed itself during both world wars.

Wartime

Through the first half of the twentieth century the reputation of English food declined, partly because of rationing. Before the First World War, Britain had become dependent on importing food. There was bacon from Denmark, lamb from New Zealand and wheat from the USA. In peacetime, there was food for all but the development of the U-boat and submarine warfare changed all that.

Rationing, however, was a great success in ensuring that everyone got sufficient food to keep the war effort going, and surprisingly, the limited diet made a lot of people eat more healthily. However, the emphasis on root vegetables made for a repetitive diet and unusual combinations such as carrot fudge were not always appealing.

Americans based in Britain were shocked by rationing and often sent home descriptions of terrible English food. One of the most unpopular features was dried eggs, imported from the USA and dried to save space on convoys. The disappointing experience of wartime dried eggs lives on in the English expression 'the dregs'.

The Modern Age

Since the end of rationing in the 1950s, English cuisine has fought hard to improve its reputation. Celebrity chefs such as Delia Smith have shown the English how to cook again. Delia even made it into the *Collins English Dictionary* with the phrase 'To do a Delia', that is, to cook in her British way. English cooks such as Heston Blumenthal have won Michelin stars for their food, with a reputation for innovative and imaginative cookery.

Celebrity chefs and reality TV programmes show that the English are now deeply interested in food, and their tastes borrow from many varied cultures.TV chefs such as Fanny Craddock, the 'Galloping Gourmet' Graham Kerr, Keith Floyd and Rick Stein have often sought French or other European influences for their cookery. Reality shows such as *Masterchef* often showcase regional delicacies from around Britain alongside influences from other parts of the world. The result is that we have many English versions of classics from other cultures and many fusions of influences.

11

GOOD SPORTS – OR NOT

The English love sports. Premier League teams such as Manchester United, Arsenal and Tottenham regularly play in front of more than 60,000 spectators. Race meetings like Ascot attract more than 200,000, spread over several days, and more than 120,000 gather at Silverstone to watch the British Formula 1 Grand Prix. Millions more watch the action on TV.

The British are also quite good at sports, being one of the few countries to have sent teams to every Summer and Winter Olympics, and we have world champions in many sports. However, one of the most significant features of the English and their sport is that many sports were invented in England, often in the late nineteenth century, and then spread around the world. This is certainly true of the only truly global team sport – football.

Sport defines the English year. From September through to May, many either play or watch football before switching to cricket through the summer. Others choose between rugby and tennis. Some sports, such as horse racing, go on all year with flat racing in the summer and jumps in the winter.

Sport provides a backdrop to the middle-class social year. In spring, families and friends gather to watch the Six Nations rugby. Around Easter, there is the University Boat Race between Oxford and Cambridge, the Grand National and the London Marathon. As summer emerges, there is Royal Ascot, followed by Wimbledon, the British Formula 1 Grand Prix and the British Open Golf Championship. All before the summer holidays.

TEN SPORTS THAT ENGLAND GAVE TO THE WORLD

1   Cricket
2   Association Football
3   Rugby (Rugby Union and Rugby League)
4   Hockey
5   Lawn and table tennis
6   Croquet
7   Badminton
8   Netball
9   Squash
10   Snooker

Cricket
There isn't much that is more English than cricket. Cricketers on a village pitch under blue summer skies, while spectators lounge in deckchairs drinking tea or sit outside a pub drinking beer, is one of the most traditional concepts of a typical English view. Perhaps first played in southern England by shepherds and their children, it is now the second-most popular spectator sport in the world.

The game may have begun in Saxon or Norman times with a shepherd's staff being used to hit a stone or ball of wool to prevent it going through the wicket, a narrow gateway. By the late seventeenth century, cricket was an adult game being played between county teams funded by wealthy aristocrats who were willing to hire 'local experts'. So much for English amateurism – cricket was already a professional sport.

Cricket matches attracted crowds and rapidly led to gambling. Early eighteenth-century press coverage focused on gambling rather than the on-field activity. Between 1770 and 1790, the press covered hundreds of cricket matches.

Rules were needed. The first Laws of Cricket were written in 1744 by the Star and Garter Club, and when the Marylebone Cricket Club was begun in 1787, it became their job to maintain and update them.

In the eighteenth century, the laws were changed to introduce a middle stump rather than a single bail placed over the outside stumps. And when a Mr White came out to bat with a bat that was wider than the stumps, laws were introduced to make the maximum width of a bat 4in.

Bowling also changed. Underarm bowling was the norm until 1760, after which bowlers were allowed to raise their arms to shoulder height. It was not until 1864 that modern overarm bowling became legal. George Simpson-Hayward was still bowling underarm for England in South Africa at the start of the twentieth century.

In 1839, Sussex became the first English county to form a club and by 1890 there was a county championship. International cricket was also under way. In 1859, a team of English professionals toured North America and in 1868 an indigenous Australian team toured England. The first England–Australia test match was played in 1889.

Yorkshire is the most successful county in the county championship with an impressive thirty-three titles – proof that it doesn't have to be hot to play cricket. Surrey, who won the first championship in 1890, are the second-most successful, with twenty-one titles.

Women's cricket is nearly as old as the men's game. The first recorded game was in 1745 in Surrey, when Hambledon defeated Bramley in a tight game won by eight notches (runs). The local press reported the 'girls bowled, batted, ran and catched [*sic*] as well as most men'. Women's cricket matches attracted large crowds, heavy gambling and even some violence.

In the nineteenth century, the White Heather Club in Nun Appleton, Yorkshire, became the first women's cricket club. In 1926, the Women's Cricket Association was founded and in the 1930s the first test was played against Australia.

Cricket is a popular sport. England has 5,000 cricket clubs, of which about 600 are women's clubs. There are just less than 300,000 cricketers in the country and 60,000 of those are women. The numbers currently playing are difficult to measure due to the disruption of the Covid pandemic.

As the British Empire spread, so did cricket. There are now eleven other nations entitled to play international test cricket. They range from Australia and New Zealand, South Africa, India, Pakistan, Bangladesh, Sri Lanka and the West Indies, where the game has long been established, to smaller nations such as Ireland, Zimbabwe and Afghanistan. Some cricket is played in a further ninety-six countries and many of these have little to do with the former British Empire. These include Uzbekistan, Ivory Coast, Serbia, Mozambique and Mongolia.

England gave cricket to the world but, of course, that doesn't mean it has always been the most successful on the pitch. In 1882, Australia defeated England at home and declared that English cricket had died – and that the body would be cremated and taken to Australia. When England toured Australia, they were presented with a small urn, containing the ashes of a wooden bail. England and Australia still compete for this urn, or a replica of it.

In 2019 England won the World Cup for the first time. Australia has been world champion five times, while India and the West Indies have both won it twice. English women have outperformed the men's team by taking four World Cups, beaten only by Australia with seven titles.

Who has made the largest contribution to women's cricket? Rachael Heyhoe-Flint is probably the most influential English women's cricketer. As captain, she never lost a test series and led

England to victory in the 1973 World Cup, a tournament she had helped to establish. Charlotte Edwards deserves mention for leading England to a World Cup triumph in 2009 and ashes successes, while Sarah Taylor, considered the best wicket keeper in the world, was good enough to hold a place in a top-level male side in Australia. However, perhaps the honour belongs with Myrtle Maclagan, who played for England in the first test against Australia. She was the first woman to score a test century and continued playing into her fifties.

It is difficult to decide who has made the biggest contribution to men's cricket in England. Was it W.G. Grace? As well as having an impressive beard, he was a master batsman, being the first to score over 300 in an innings. Or Sir Jack Hobbs? He scored a record 199 centuries in a career interrupted by the First World War. What about Sir Len Hutton, who scored a record 364 for England in his sixth test? Or the 'Fiery' Fred Trueman, who became the first bowler to take 300 wickets? There is, of course, Sir Ian Botham of Ashes fame. And Sir Alastair Cook is England's leading run scorer in tests. Or what about James Anderson, who is still playing? The number of 'Sirs' in the list tells you something about their impact on the country.

Football

When it was suggested to him that football was a matter of life and death, Bill Shankly famously replied that it was more important than that. And, yes, Shankly was a Scot, but he was talking about a game mostly invented in England.

There were early versions of football across the globe but the modern game is acknowledged to have begun in England in the nineteenth century. Major public schools, Rugby, Eton, Charterhouse and Harrow, all had their own versions of football games, which were played within the schools. There was great enthusiasm for football games in England at this time but without a set of agreed rules, opportunities for matches between different schools and clubs were few.

The oldest football club still playing is Sheffield FC, founded in 1857. Ebenezer Morley, a solicitor and founder of Barnes FC, wrote a letter to a newspaper suggesting that a Football Association (FA) should be formed to agree a set of rules as had happened in cricket. In 1863, representatives from a dozen London clubs met and eventually agreed a set of rules. The names of the clubs represented give an insight into who was playing the game at this time. There was a Civil Service FC, Crusaders, Crystal Palace, Kennington School, and even a No Names Club.

After much dispute, the FA was formed and rules written. Handling of the ball was not entirely banned, and a fair catch was defined. If the task of the meeting was to unite the footballing world, it was an initial failure. Many clubs who favoured Rugby rules did not attend and Blackheath refused to accept FA rules. By 1871, Rugby rules clubs had formed the RFU instead, as we will see shortly.

In 1871–72, the FA organised the first FA Cup. Twelve teams competed and Wanderers beat the Royal Engineers to be the first winners. It was a race to see whether Association Football would prove more popular than its Rugby Union rival. Over fifty clubs competed in the FA cup in 1877 and 100 by 1883–84. Association Football had won the race.

The key to FA success was accepting professionalism. As factories began to give workers a half-day on Saturday, more people were able to play football and to watch it. As crowds increased and spectators were prepared to pay to watch, it was inevitable that players would begin to be paid. In 1885, the FA decided to allow clubs to field professionals and in 1888 the first football league appeared with twelve teams. Founder members included some familiar names – Aston Villa, Everton, Blackburn Rovers, Bolton Wanderers, Wolves and West Bromwich Albion. By 1913, 121,000 spectators gathered to watch the FA Cup Final. It was clear that football was a commercial success.

In spreading football across the world, the English had quite a lot of help from the Scots, who were also keen to export the game and their effective short-passing tactics. Football spread through the Empire as a way for cricketers to keep fit in the winter season. In Canada and neighbouring USA, grid-iron football and rugby provided alternative entertainment, while in Australia they already had their own form of football and New Zealand preferred rugby. In India, local football teams were eager to show that they could play the game as well as the English and in Nigeria, football success became a way of campaigning for independence.

Football was an easy game to spread, requiring little specialist equipment beyond a ball. In Argentina it was railway engineers as well as merchants who helped spread the game; in Mexico it was Cornish miners; in Korea it was the navy and in the Middle East it was oil workers or the army. Within Europe the game was often spread by locals who had picked up the game alongside their education in England. Spain, France, Italy and Germany all learned the game from England and now we mostly learn how to play the game from them.

English women have also acted as inspiration for others wanting to play football around the world. In 1881, the Scottish suffragist Helen Matthews organised a game in Edinburgh against English women. The Scots won 3–0, but the English triumphed in a later game on English soil. Two of the four-match series were interrupted by crowd violence.

Women's football was revived during the First World War as women in northern England played football matches to raise money for the war effort. The teams were often factory teams and matches attracted crowds of up to 10,000. The leading team was Dick Kerr Ladies, managed by Albert Frankland, using workers from Dick Kerr Munitions. In the 1920s, Dick Kerr and his team, including star Lily Parr, toured in France and the USA showing what women could achieve on the football pitch. To its shame, the FA disagreed with what was going on and banned women's football in 1921; a ban that was to remain in force for fifty years.

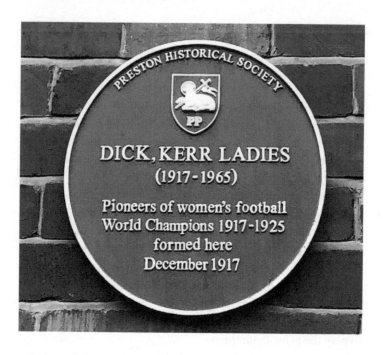

PRESTON HISTORICAL SOCIETY

PP

DICK, KERR LADIES
(1917-1965)

Pioneers of women's football
World Champions 1917-1925
formed here
December 1917

'Football's coming home' – the anthem is sung in pubs and on terraces every couple of years in the hope that England will triumph at either a World Cup or a European Championship. The triumph of Alf Ramsey, Bobby Moore, Bobby Charlton and Geoff Hurst in 1966 is the only major success in either for the England men's team. However, the Lionesses triumphed at the 2022 Women's Euros.

England's Premier League is the richest and most watched league in the world. It is an international league in the sense that many teams feature few English players. No English manager has won the Premier League and the last English manager to triumph in the top flight of English football was Howard Wilkinson in 1991–92.

Which is the best football club in England? Obviously, it's the one you support.

Rugby

The story is that, in 1823, William Webb Ellis, a pupil at Rugby School, caught the ball in a football match and called a mark. Instead of kicking the ball, as was the rule at the time, he picked up the ball and ran with it. He died in 1872, completely unaware that he was the inventor of rugby.

The story did not fully emerge until later in the 1870s and only really gained ground in 1895, when rugby was splitting between public school southerners and northern workers. The northern clubs broke away from the Rugby Football Union (RFU) and a professional Rugby League emerged with players paid to play. Rugby Union, the (at that stage) amateur game, adopted the Webb Ellis story because it was keen to publicise itself as a game for gentlemen. Even now it is a professional game, the World Cup trophy still carries the Webb Ellis name.

There are similarities between rugby and medieval folk football, played not only in England but elsewhere in the world, from Australia to China. The modern game began in public schools such as Rugby in the nineteenth century, where football was popular, and each school had its own set of rules. In 1845, three teenagers, William Arnold (son of previous headmaster, Thomas Arnold), W. Shirley and Frederick Hutchins, codified Rugby's football rules. Rugby alumni wanted to continue playing once they left school and began to start football clubs, as did alumni from other private schools.

As we have seen, in 1863 the FA was formed with the intention of producing a single set of football rules. The association was unable to reach agreement on whether hacking opponents was a legitimate tactic and whether players could run with the ball once they had caught it. Blackheath Club took exception to hacking being banned as they thought it would ruin the essence of the game and they left the FA and took with them those clubs who favoured hacking and running with the ball.

In 1871, twenty-one London clubs who opposed FA rules met in Pall Mall to form the RFU and see if they could agree on their own set of rules. Unsurprisingly, three Rugby alumni, Rutter, Holmes and Maton, got the job of writing the new rules and, as they were all lawyers, those rules became laws. The leading Premier League club Harlequins was at the initial meeting, while it is said that Wasps missed out on being founder members by turning up at the wrong pub on the wrong day.

Current Premier League Rugby Union clubs have a long history. All were in existence by the end of the nineteenth century. Bath, Harlequins, Sale and Wasps started in the 1860s; Exeter, Saracens, Gloucester, Worcester and Newcastle in the 1870s; Northampton, Leicester and Bristol in the 1880s and London Irish in the 1890s. However, the game they played was very different from modern professional rugby.

Hacking, the practice that had forced Blackheath out of the FA, was banned in 1871. The game was twenty players per side until 1877. Until 1888, the result was decided by the number of goals scored. A try was worth nothing, but it did allow you to have a try at kicking a goal. Kicks could be charged down and the ball was in play as soon as the kicker placed the ball, so there was no opportunity for a full Jonny Wilkinson routine. The ball itself was a pig's bladder inflated by mouth like a balloon, a job requiring willing volunteers. The size was not defined until 1892 and earlier models were easier to kick than to throw.

Rugby was quick to spread through the Empire. Rugby football was developing in Australia almost at the same time as it was in England and Tom Wills, who developed Australian football, was educated at Rugby. In the USA and Canada, rugby competed for attention alongside grid-iron football.

The army, Cornish miners and missionaries combined to introduce the game in South Africa and in New Zealand the oldest rugby club was founded in 1863. Outside the Empire, Argentina had a rugby championship before the end of the nineteenth century. It's amazing how quickly the game spread without the internet or even fixed telephone lines.

Women were already playing rugby in the late nineteenth century and international rugby appeared as soon as the RFU was formed with an international against Scotland in 1871. By 1882, there was an annual international competition between England, Scotland, Wales and Ireland and by 1987 there was a World Cup.

Rugby League, which was professional when Rugby Union was still determinedly amateur, has also spread across the world. In the 2021 Rugby League World Cup (held in 2022 because of Covid), teams from sixteen nations took part in the men's event, with eight teams each taking part in the women's tournament and the wheelchair tournament.

England admires its rugby heroes for their determination and strength of character under pressure. Jonny Wilkinson became BBC Sports Personality of the Year in 2003 for the drop kick that won the World Cup. The winning captain, Martin Johnson, was the runner-up.

Hockey

Hockey (the type played on an unfrozen surface) is the second-most popular team sport in the world. It is played in 137 countries by 30 million players and is enjoyed by both men and women. England, and in particular English public schools, played an important role in starting this popular sport.

England did not invent the idea of hitting a ball with a stick. Similar ball and stick games were played by the Greeks, Romans and Persians as well as the Aztecs. In the UK, Ireland has hurling and Scotland has shinty.

The game appeared, like football, in English schools in the nineteenth century and some chose to continue playing once they left school. Blackheath was the first club, in 1861, and by 1875 there were seven London clubs. As in football, there were often disputes about which rules to use. In 1875, the Hockey Association was founded, and the first set of rules was introduced. The game was to be played with a ball rather than a rubber cube, sticks had to remain below the shoulder and goals had to be scored from within the circle. The basis of the modern game was established.

The British Army took the game to India, where it became very popular. Men's hockey appeared in the 1908 Olympics and has been a permanent feature since 1928. At home, women took up the game in the nineteenth century and, initially, played friendly matches. In England, there are more than 800 clubs and almost 150,000 players. Both British men and women's teams have won Olympic gold – the men at Seoul in 1988 and the women at Rio in 2016.

Tennis

'Every time Wimbledon is on, I am thinking, "Yes, I could do the same" and get out the racket. Sadly, not the same results.'

Kate Middleton

In late June and early July, much of Middle England feels the same as the Princess of Wales. Some will queue overnight to drink Pimm's, eat strawberries and cream and watch the matches. Some will be glued to the TV and others will be inspired to have a game on a local court.

The Lawn Tennis Association estimates that about 4 million people in England and Wales pick up a racket at least once per year. Tennis is important to the English but it's really more of a cultural and historical affection rather than based on actual sporting success.

Andy Murray is the only Brit to win Wimbledon in the open era and is clearly the star of British tennis. He has won two consecutive Olympic golds and won the US Open twice. He is though, of course, a proud Scot.

Emma Raducanu has already won the US Open and BBC Sports Personality, but she is still very young and may, or may not, go on to even greater achievements. It is some time since we have had other major English tennis stars.

Angela Mortimer won three Grand Slam singles titles between 1955 and 1961, Ann Haydon Jones won three in the 1960s and Virginia Wade won three between 1968 and 1977. English men have been less successful than the women. The outstanding character is Fred Perry, who won all the Grand Slam tournaments in the 1930s, including three Wimbledons on the trot.

Tennis began in France in the Middle Ages with a game called *jeu de paume*, played by monks, which developed into real tennis, as played by Henry VIII. The name 'tennis' may derive from the French *tenez*, meaning 'take or receive' – a warning shouted by the server to his opponent as he struck the ball. Although popular in the sixteenth century, the game had largely died out by the nineteenth century.

The modern game of tennis was invented in England in the nineteenth century and there are two possible inventors, one English and the other Welsh. The official verdict goes to the Welshman Major Walter Clopton Wingfield, who published a set of rules in 1873, and tennis celebrated its centenary in 1973. Wingfield's game was to be played on an hourglass-shaped court with vulcanised rubber balls. He patented the court and marketed tennis sets, which included rackets, balls and nets, along with instructions on how to play.

The English contender was Major Harry Gem and his friend Augurio Perera from Spain. They invented a game based on a mixture of Gem's favourite game rackets and Perera's knowledge of pelota and played it on a croquet lawn. In 1872, the pair established a tennis club in Leamington.

Five years later, the All-England Croquet Club in Wimbledon decided to set aside some of its lawns for a tennis championship. Consequently, they drew up some rules: an oblong court rather than an hourglass one, the introduction of the real tennis system of scoring – 15, 30, 40, game and two chances to serve. Lawn tennis was born.

The rules and court dimensions are relatively unchanged, despite improvements in equipment. The All-England Club added tennis to its title, and Wimbledon is still one of the Grand Slam tournaments.

Tennis spread rapidly around the world as Wingfield's boxes of equipment were easy to ship. By 1880, there was a US championship and by 1905 an Australian one as well. The French championship was established in 1891, but only for the French. It became an international tournament in 1925. All four Grand Slams were in place within fifty years. Now there are nearly 90 million tennis players worldwide and courts in nearly every country. Another English (and Welsh) export.

Table Tennis

Lawn tennis's smaller indoor brother was another English sporting invention. It was invented in 1890 by David Foster, who filed a patent for his game of indoor tennis on a table. It was a game played with a rubber ball and strung rackets. The equipment also included side netting to prevent stray balls causing damage. There had been earlier versions, with wealthy gentlemen apparently shaping champagne corks into balls, using cigar boxes as bats and books as nets. It all sounds a bit of a faff.

The game was revolutionised in the early years of the twentieth century when Englishman James Gibb brought celluloid balls back from the USA. Another Englishman, E.C. Gould, introduced wooden bats with rubberised pimples, allowing the ball to be spun.

The first world championship was held in London in 1926 and Fred Perry liked to play the game. In 1988 it became an Olympic sport. Today, it is played in 200 countries and there are over 260 million players. This English invention has a claim to being one of the world's most popular sports.

Croquet

The lawns of the All-England Club were home to croquet before tennis. It is worth considering croquet as another sport that was discovered, marketed, codified and exported by Victorian England. The name sounds French, and the game may have originated in thirteenth-century France. It seems to have spread to Ireland, where it became known as 'crooky'.

In the nineteenth century the game came to England, and it was turned into a sport. It was featured in the 1851 Great Exhibition and appeared in Lewis Carroll's *Alice in Wonderland*.

In 1857, John Jaques wrote a set of rules and marketed croquet sets. His firm remains the leading manufacturer of croquet equipment. The sets spread rapidly across the British Empire in the 1870s and 65,000 copies of the rules were published in England. Croquet appeared in the Paris Olympics in 1900.

The sport is less popular now, but England still has about 150 croquet clubs, catering for between 5,500 and 10,000 players. Many more enjoy the game outside clubs. Croquet is played in about thirty countries including Uruguay, Japan, Latvia and Switzerland. A bit of a niche sport, perhaps, but still fun and significant.

Badminton

Another racket game that appeared in England in the nineteenth century was badminton. Its origins go back to a game called battledore, which was played in Greece, Egypt, China and India. The battledore was the bat and shuttlecocks were often made from cork and feathers. There was no net, and the aim of the game was simply to keep a rally going for as many strokes as possible.

The British Army came across the game in India and in 1850 introduced the idea of a net. The game changed its name to Poona, named after an army base, where it was popular. Army officers then brought the game back to England. It was played by the Duke of Beaufort at his country estate, Badminton House, and the sport has been known as badminton ever since.

In 1893, the Badminton Association of England was formed, and the modern rules were codified. England was one of the nine founding members of the International Badminton Association in 1934. France, the Netherlands and Denmark were also members, showing that the sport had grown beyond the confines of the British Empire.

Badminton is now a global sport, played in over 150 countries, and tends to be dominated by China. Badminton England claims that over 3 million adults in the country play at least once per year and over 4,000 participate in its competitions. In 2006, English players Nathan Robertson and Gail Emms took the mixed doubles title in the Badminton World Championships.

Netball

England Netball estimates that about 160,000 women play the game once per week during the season, making it the most popular women's game after football. Its popularity is on the rise after England's success at the 2018 Commonwealth Games. There is also a men's version of the game, 'Net'. Around the world there are 20 million players in well over 100 countries.

England was involved in inventing the game and was responsible for spreading it across the world through the Empire. It remains very popular in the Commonwealth.

Netball has its origins in women's basketball. Canadian James Naismith invented basketball in Massachusetts in 1891 when instructed to invent a safe indoor game for young men at the YMCA. Clara Baer modified basketball for women and this spread across the USA.

Women's basketball soon crossed the Atlantic. The game was adapted to be played outdoors where the basketball hoops had no backboards. Players were not allowed to dribble. The Physical Education Association wrote a set of rules in 1901 and netball had been created.

An All-England Net Ball Association emerged between the wars and national competitions were played. After the Second World War, international matches were arranged, leading to the first world championship in England in 1963. The International Netball Federation remains based in England.

Squash

Squash is played in 185 countries by 20 million players and is being considered for the 2028 Olympics. It was invented at Harrow School in the late nineteenth century from the older sports of racquets and fives.

Racquets began in the eighteenth century at London's debtor's gaol, the Fleet. Real tennis was modified to hitting a ball against one or two walls. The golf ball-sized ball was made from tightly wound cloth and the racquet was a modified real tennis one. The game spread through England and across the Empire with specialist courts being built.

Fives was a form of handball played in public schools such as Eton, Rugby and Harrow. Similar to racquets, but without a bat, the ball was struck by a gloved hand. The emergence of vulcanised rubber in the 1840s led to the creation of new softer and slower balls. When Harrow School opened a new racquets and fives complex in 1864, boys used some of the fives courts to play racquets with the slower, softer ball and 'soft racquets', or squash, was properly born.

The sport spread slowly from Harrow to other schools and some enthusiasts built their own courts at home. Gurney Burton built one at Catton Hall in Norwich for £360 in 1882, and by 1905 there were also courts at Lord's and Queens Club. However, in the period before the First World War there was no agreement about what size a court should be or what type of ball could be used. It was not until 1928 that the Squash Rackets Association (England Squash) agreed on the size of a court.

Deciding on a suitable ball was going to take much longer. In the USA, players favoured a hard, fast ball, while in England the search was for a slower, softer ball. Eventually, the softball version of squash became the recognised version of the sport.

In 1967, the International Squash Rackets Federation was formed by Australia, UK, Egypt, India, New Zealand, Pakistan and South Africa. Its headquarters remains in England. England Squash estimates that there are 200,000 English players. We have World Open winners such as Nick Matthew, Cassie Campion and Laura Massaro. We should also remember 'Mr Squash', Jonah Barrington, who helped make the sport professional in the 1970s.

Snooker

While billiards originated as a French game – an indoor, table version of croquet – it was being played here in England by the sixteenth century and Shakespeare makes a reference to it. Snooker, by contrast, is a modern game invented by Neville Chamberlain (not the Chamberlain of 'Peace with honour' fame) as a young army officer in India in 1875. Lieutenant Chamberlain took the game of 'black pool', played with fifteen reds and a black, and added the yellow, green, brown, blue and pink. Cadets at the Royal Military Academy in Woolwich were nicknamed 'Snookers', and as they watched and played Chamberlain's game, it took the name snooker.

Billiards champion John Roberts was introduced to snooker by Chamberlain and popularised the game in England. The first amateur championship took place during the First World War. Joe Davis helped to make snooker professional and won the first of his fifteen world championships in 1927. In 1969, the BBC series *Pot Black* made snooker players superstars.

All but three world champions have been from the UK. Joe's brother, Fred Davis, John Pullman, Ronnie O'Sullivan and Steve Davis have all won more than five championships each.

SOME OTHER SPORTS THAT ENGLISH PEOPLE HAVE BEEN PRETTY GOOD AT

So far, we have been looking at sports that began in England or where England played an important role in developing it. However, the English don't just like the sports they made, they are pretty good at quite a lot of others as well.

Athletics
The most popular individual sport in England is running, with about 5 per cent of people running once a week. And England has a proud history of success in athletics generally. Charles Bennett from Dorset became the first Brit to win an Olympic Gold medal in the 1,500m in 1900. Mary Rand was the first British woman to win an Olympic track-and-field event, winning the long jump in 1964.

Britain's most successful track athlete was born Hussein Abdi Kahin, in Mogadishu Somalia, but is better known as Mo Farah, with four golds in the 5,000m and 10,000m. England has done particularly well at the 800m and 1,500m. Albert Hill won both in 1920, a feat repeated by Kelly Holmes in 2004 in Athens. Douglas Lowe won the 800m at both 1924 and 1928 Olympics, while Seb Coe won the 1500m in 1980 and 1984. Daley Thompson won two gold medals for the decathlon in 1980 and 1984 and George Larnar won both the 3,500m walk and the 10-mile walk in 1908. Overall, Britain is the third-most successful track-and-field nation at the Olympics, with fifty-five golds, eighty silvers and seventy bronzes.

The BBC Sports Personality of the Year gives an impression of which sporting achievements are most admired by the great British public. Athletics has provided more winners than any other sport, which shows its place in our hearts.

Rowing

Rowing seems very English, considering the Oxford and Cambridge Boat Race, *Three Men in a Boat* and so on. England also has a long history of Olympic success with rowing.

Britain won its first medal in 1900, when rowing made its debut. Between 1984 and 2016 we won thirty-one gold medals for rowing. Leading the way was Sir Steve Redgrave, who won gold in five consecutive Olympics, often partnered by Sir Matthew Pinsent, who won four golds. The most successful women were Helen Glover and Heather Stanning, both of whom have a pair of gold medals.

Cycling

Since the National Lottery started funding British Cycling in 1996, cycling here has also had a lot of Olympic success. Top of the pile are the married couple Jason and Laura Kenny. Jason won seven gold medals and a silver between 2008 and 2020, while Laura won five golds in the 2012, 2016 and 2021 Olympics – enough medals for a small country let alone one family. Ed Clancy won gold at three separate Olympics in 2008, 2012 and 2016, while Victoria Pendleton, Benjamin Jones, Steven Burke, Philip Hindes, Clarence Kingsbury and Joana Rowsel-Shand all won a couple of gold medals each.

British cycling has also had a good record on the road. Bradley Wiggins (born in Ghent, grew up in England) won the Tour de France in 2012 and also has five Olympic gold medals, making him a strong contender for Britain's greatest-ever cyclist. Chris Froome (born to English parents in Kenya and grew up there

and in South Africa) has won four Tour de France, the Giro d'Italia and the Vuelta a España (twice). Mark Cavendish (born on the Isle of Man) has been a world champion and equalled Eddy Merckx's record of Tour de France stage wins.

For a born-in-England, world-famous English cyclist, you have to look towards Chris Boardman, who held a world record for the mile on the track but was less successful on the road. Tom Simpson, who won races such as the Milan–San Remo and a world professional road race title before his sad end on Mont Ventoux, deserves a mention here. And obviously there is Simon Yates, who won the Vuelta a España in 2018.

Formula 1 Motor Racing (F1)
England has a proud tradition in F1 motor racing. Six of the ten teams are based in the UK and England has numerous F1 world champions. Mike Hawthorn was the first English F1 champion in 1958. He was followed by John Surtees in 1964 and James Hunt in 1976, Nigel Mansell (1992), Damon Hill (1996) and Jenson Button in 2009. Graham Hill managed a pair of world championships in 1962 and 1968, while Lewis

Hamilton has a record-equalling seven world championships. Every English supporter knows he deserved an eighth title in 2021. Surprisingly, the most famous English racing driver, Stirling Moss, never won the world championship although he did win sixteen Grand Prix races.

Perhaps even more significant than any individual driver was the contribution of Bernie Ecclestone. Ecclestone made his money as a car salesman, before buying the Brabham racing team. He went on to form and lead the Formula One Constructors' Association and, pretty much ran F1 until he sold it in 2016. He turned a small European-dominated sport into a world phenomenon.

12

RANDOM THOUGHTS ON BEING ENGLISH TODAY

We know a lot about how England and the English got to be where we are today. We, of course, know very little about where the English will be in a century or two. It would be nice to think we will still exist in some form, but something history tells us plainly is that predicting the distant future is more than a bit hard.

Anyone writing a *Little Book of England* two centuries ago is unlikely to have predicted the end of the British Empire, a world where the global superpowers are China and the USA, curry is one of our favourite dishes, and where we won a football World Cup in 1966 but haven't won it since. So, rather than worrying too much about what the future might bring, we are going to end this book with a few thoughts on what it's like being English today.

Admittedly, some of those adhering to the understated view of what it means to be English would argue that asking what it means to be English is something that's very unEnglish! Plus, there is the fact that some people who are regarded as English by others don't necessarily regard themselves as very English. There are those, for example, who choose to identify themselves as British, rather than English. For some, the terms are interchangeable, and it depends on whether it's a World Cup year or an Olympic year!

We have also seen that England has strong regional identities in terms of food, language and dialects. For many, this regional identity – Yorkshire, Geordie or Londoner, for instance – is as powerful as our national character, or even more so. However, this is the *Little Book of England*, so let's have a look at what we can say about being English.

For a start, we are known the world over. This can be a benefit; few people, anywhere in the world, have never heard of England. So, if you tell someone you are English, you are not going to get people sounding confused and saying, 'Where?' Although, obviously, England isn't called England in everybody else's language, so there is still some scope for confusion. In French, England is *Angleterre*; in Spanish, it's *Inglaterra*. However, if you try out assorted versions of Engl-, Angl-, Ingl-, a lot of people in a lot of places will finally work out where you are from.

Having said that, people immediately knowing where you are from can also have its problems, because being English can bring a lot of historical baggage. If you end up in one of the very many places the English have invaded or colonised over the centuries, and where there is still resentment, arriving waving a St George's flag and shouting, 'WE'RE ENGLISH! WE'RE BACK!' would be unwise. Some English people in such situations have pretended to be Welsh, Scottish or Irish. Not everybody in the world knows where Wales, Scotland and Ireland are, but they are clearly not England.

Having a long and (often) distinguished history is sometimes one of the good bits of being English. England is the land of Magna Carta, Shakespeare, the Beatles; a land that has contributed hugely to the world's culture. Being English, it is fun to think that, in some sense, you are part of all this.

On the other hand, times change. A hundred years ago, most English people would have viewed as heroes those Englishmen and Englishwomen who helped to build the British Empire. Views of the Empire today are very much more mixed. There is much more acknowledgement of the pain and suffering it caused. And England's involvement in slavery and the slave trade is perhaps the most shameful part of our history.

Having a long and well-known history can also cause problems for a nation's future. When previous generations of English men and women have achieved so much, it can seem harder to appreciate the achievements of present and future generations. English people sometimes seem to find it difficult to accept that England is not quite the global force it once was. English politicians can seem fascinated with the idea of imitating Churchill or Thatcher (or, in fact, imitating some selected parts of these two politicians), rather than creating new approaches that are better suited to the twenty-first century. English football fans still dream of 1966 and there is still some kind of expectation that today's England teams should match that huge achievement. The recent triumph of the England women at Wembley in the Euros has not fully slaked the 1966 thirst.

In the search for life on planets beyond our solar system, there is the concept of the Goldilocks Zone. This is, of course, a reference to Goldilocks, the Three Bears and all that porridge. There was porridge that was too hot, porridge that was too cold, and porridge that was just right. The Goldilocks Zone for exoplanets is the zone where temperatures are right for water to remain liquid. A lot of English people (and some others) have, over the centuries, viewed England and the English as occupying a sort of geographical and cultural Goldilocks Zone.

It is not, of course, news to anyone that England is in a zone where the temperature is usually right for water to remain liquid. Globally, England is probably more famous for being wet than the wettest part of any tropical rainforest. Travelling across the world, if you say you are from England and that it has rained a lot there, you will often get a ready grin of recognition.

England does generally have a moderate climate, which is not too cold and not too hot, and (despite its reputation) not too wet and not too dry. Sometimes (usually on a warm, dry, pleasant, spring or summer day with the countryside lush and green and with bright flowers to be seen) we English do genuinely appreciate our climate. Some English people, when they see stories of weather disasters around the world, feel a little relieved about the climate here.

However, we also spend a lot of time complaining about the weather being too hot or too cold, or too wet or too dry. And then we spend a lot of money going on holiday to places that are hotter and drier than here. It may or may not be a coincidence that a lot of the places around the world that were invaded by English people also have warmer climates than here. For example, historically, English people have spent more time invading southern Europe and Africa than they have invading Scandinavia. However, those English people who enjoy winter sports do also spend a lot of money going to places that are much colder than here.

Traditionally, it has been thought that in addition to this atmospheric moderation there is also an emotional moderation in England. A lot of English people have, over the centuries, looked around the world at people getting angry and decided that England, by contrast, is a land of moderate emotions, an emotional Goldilocks zone. In this zone, so the theory goes, English people are not too dull and boring, and not too excitable and angry, but are 'just right'.

It is far beyond the remit of this little book to measure the emotional climate of all the countries of the entire world. In reality, just as is true of the populations of all other countries, some English people are dull and boring, some are excitable and angry, some are emotionally moderate, and most vary quite a lot depending on what's going on in their lives.

As we have already seen in this book, there have been a lot of angry English people throughout English history and, as a nation, we don't seem to be getting any less angry. There were a lot of angry people on both sides in the arguments over Brexit, and newspaper stories regularly describe 'outrage' over a wide variety of sometimes minor irritations. Our keenness for orderly queuing is often described as a sign of English moderation but, if you want to see genuine anger, watch what happens when somebody fails to observe queue etiquette and joins it somewhere apart from the end of the queue.

'Fair play' is also an important concept to the English. The phrase itself goes back to Shakespeare and is still widely used. In a broader sense, the concept is still a defining feature of how the English like to feel they resolve disputes and deal with life and sport, and the phrase is more commonly used here than in other parts of the English-speaking world.

However, winning (in sport, in politics, in war etc.) has also been important to the English for a very long time. We have been very good at it, and it has made England among the richest and (arguably) most successful nations in the world. However, it would be fair to say that it has not always been achieved fairly. Not all foreigners associate England and the English with fair play. The phrase 'perfidious Albion' has been widely

used in Europe over the centuries to describe a rather less than admiring view of England's and Britain's approach to fair play in the international sphere. In a sporting sense, fair play has, to a great extent, been superseded in professional competitive sport and, even in amateur days, icons such as W.G. Grace were well known for intimidating umpires.

There is perhaps a little more value in the argument that England has managed to develop a significant degree of moderation in some of its political, religious and cultural institutions. It is historical fact that England has, since the end of the Civil War in the seventeenth century, suffered less internal political, religious and cultural violence than many countries around the world. However, the reasons for that are many and complex and do not seem based on anything uniquely English.

Yes, there is widespread respect for law and order in England, but England is not alone in that respect, and it would be unwise to assume that England will forever, in the future, avoid major political, religious or cultural violence. In addition, one major reason that there was less violence here in the eighteenth, nineteenth and twentieth centuries was that Englishmen and women were colonising other countries and not allowing other countries to colonise England.

During the period of the British Empire, a lot of English people acquired an admiration for the Roman Empire, seeing similarities between the two. Across the British Empire, major government buildings were constructed with classical design features that made some kind of architectural link between the two empires. The main frontage of the Bank of England looks like some enormous Roman temple. Novels were written and, in the twentieth century, films and TV programmes were made in which Roman officers seemed quite English.

Yet the Roman Empire was in many senses a Mediterranean Empire. Yes, it controlled lands in northern Europe and in the east, in places such as what is now Iraq. But its core was the lands in Europe, Asia and Africa that bordered the Mediterranean.

And there is an element among the English and an element in Englishness that defines itself in contrast to past and present Mediterranean culture. You can holiday in Greece or Spain, drink Spanish beer and Italian wine and drive a French or Italian car and still not see yourself as closely linked to Mediterranean culture.

In the twentieth century, many English people embraced, in addition to their English identities, a British identity and then a European identity. The increasing diversity of populations within England in the late twentieth and twenty-first centuries, particularly with the growth of major communities of African, Caribbean and Asian heritage, has gently changed the nature of Englishness. Yet, there is an element of Englishness (not only seen in those whose ancestors have been in England for centuries) that contains some very traditional north European features. Individually, these features are not unique to northern Europe, but there is something in the combination of them that perhaps seems quite traditional in that region.

Some level of cultural sophistication is seen as good, but too much cultural sophistication is viewed with a little suspicion. Drinking alcohol is a part of most social occasions, and an ability to drink a lot of alcohol is viewed as an asset. Strong women are a source of pride. There is an enthusiasm for wildness and fun. There is a sort of warrior culture devotion to the armed forces. There is passionate loyalty to the monarch and monarchy.

We are not saying that, for instance, a pride in strong women is something uniquely English. It clearly isn't unique to England. Nor are we saying that you have to drink a lot and love the king, to be a good English person. Clearly you don't.

However, it is interesting that this set of values is something that would have been familiar to many of the inhabitants of the early kingdoms in Britain all those centuries ago. Will Englishmen and women two centuries from now still hold such values? Nobody knows. These future English people may (very wisely) have reduced their alcohol intake. But let's hope they at least retain the enthusiasm for wildness and fun!